NOT OF REASON

Caitlin Press Inc.
8100 Alderwood Road
Halfmoon Bay, BC V0N 1Y1
www.caitlin-press.com

Text and cover design by Vici Johnstone
Cover image: Amber McLaughlin
Printed in Canada

Caitlin Press Inc. acknowledges financial support from the Government of Canada and the Canada Council for the Arts, and the Province of British Columbia through the British Columbia Arts Council and the Book Publisher's Tax Credit.

Library and Archives Canada Cataloguing in Publication

Not of reason : a recipe for outrunning sadness / Rita Moir.
Moir, Rita, 1952- author.
Canadiana 20210200952 | ISBN 9781773860633 (softcover)
LCSH: Moir, Rita, 1952- | LCSH: Moir, Rita, 1952-—Family. | CSH: Authors, Canadian (English)—Biography. | CSH: Authors, Canadian (English)—Family relationships. | LCSH: Heart—Surgery—Patients— Family relationships. | LCSH: Mothers—Death. | LCSH: Sisters—Death. | LCSH: Bereavement. | LCGFT: Autobiographies.
LCC PS8576.O3755 Z46 2021 | DDC C818/.5403—dc23

Not of REASON

A RECIPE FOR OUTRUNNING SADNESS

RITA MOIR

CAITLIN PRESS 2021

For my sister, Judy McLaughlin, and my mother,
Erin (Edna Mae) Moir

For their ethics and smarts, laughter and hospitality
(in its true meaning), sheer guts and grace

Contents

Prologue: 2012

Easter Sunday, April 8

I take Brier, my golden retriever, for a walk on the rail line that winds through the forest by the river. It's another sunny day of Easter, the second after so many days of gloom. I remove my heavy sweatshirt and sit on a bench as Brier heads to the water. It's her first spring, and every part of the world is her mystery to explore. I close my eyes to feel the sun; no one comes by and my breathing slows.

It's the first Easter since my sister died and I crave silence. I had tried for the company of voices, but the giggling host on the radio annoyed me. I tried a violin concerto, but it distracted me. Gospel choir, perfect for a Sunday, this particular Sunday, the Montreal Jubilation Choir, but it was too much. I want the sound of Brier gnawing her bone, the snap of the woodstove as the metal heats, the bark of a distant dog. I want the heat of spring sun melting the cold of the blue sky two days past the full moon. I want nothing productive, just this time alone to watch the daffodils push through sodden and icy leaf mulch, just this time to watch a young dog play at the river's edge.

In our rural valley in British Columbia, we are perhaps more "hands on" in the rituals of death than in other places. Yesterday, for example, we stood in our graveyard in the mountains burying the ashes and saying farewell to a young man who grew up here in the Slocan Valley.

In our community hall, his parents and friends set up for his memorial as I finished cleaning after the previous night's dance. On the piano, they placed his photos and the music he had written. They hauled in casseroles and salads and cakes covered in tin foil and labelled with people's names. They set the tables with long green cloths; they spread flowered cloths angled just so across the middle. Small vases of daffodils, large vases of dried grasses and cedar boughs, and daffodils again. I reminded them how to turn on the big gas stove, how to use the dishwasher, then left them to their tasks.

We deepen and deepen, each time we celebrate a birth, or, after a death dig the spade into the frozen ground at our cemetery, where this young man's mother and father stand quietly in overcoats and boots; we know each other's stories, or we take this time to learn more, to simply show up to help with the lifting and moving on.

A large bell made by a local metal worker hangs low. After the Buddhist ceremony, each mourner kneels on the cedar boughs that cover the ashes. We strike the bell and remain kneeling as the reverberation sings, until the forest is quiet, as if his spirit has lifted.

———

The walk with Brier by the river is the perfect silence I've been seeking. There is only the river still quiet before runoff, the silence of sun in blue sky, the golden of old grasses, the dog looking up at me as she exalts in the water below.

It goes like this, the saying: in the natural order, parents should die before their children. But that fairy tale of natural order is only a candle held to the dark. When, really, has it ever been true? Not yesterday at our cemetery. Not in the great epidemics, not in the huge sweep of poverty or the gutting of war, not even in middle-class families with all the privileges of good health care. It is not the natural order in my family. Not the natural order in many families I know. I could recite a dozen instances of children dying before parents, three in my immediate family, four if we include my extended family, six if we go back another generation. Many of my friends have lost their children: Amanda, Penny and Larry's baby; Lois and Craig's son, Jesse; Dale and Tara's son, Zack; crib deaths, cancer, a child who simply didn't wake up. My partner Dan's daughter, Teri, and now this young man, Wilson Padmos, whose ashes lie beneath the bell. A few days ago, my friend Mitzi told me the third of her four adult sons had just died. They died in the order in which they were born. What natural order is that? I go down the backroads and lanes of memory, up the rows of gravestones of children young and old, who died before their parents.

———

As I sit in the sun on a bench by the Slocan River, next to a small bed of yellow crocuses, Brier paws for minnows. I've seen all our family dogs do this. They are curious and naive and brave all at once. Brier dunks her head and shakes it in surprise, then tackles the river harder, plunges, rear end in the air.

"Brier, what are you doing?" I call in alarm. She is too young and can't swim, let alone stay underwater so long. She ignores me; her head's far under and the water flies and her tail wags as she digs at the riverbed.

Dragging up a trapped and bedraggled branch, she raises her eyes to mine, triumphant.

———

The unnatural order has not spared my family: my sister Donna had a baby who after heart surgery died at the age of one month. My sister Judy's son William was killed at age twenty-three in a plane crash. Judy's stepson John died of a brain tumour at forty-one. And in the continuation of this unnatural order, after Judy and my elderly mother each had heart surgery during the same week, my mother was alive a year later and my sister, at age sixty-six, was dead.

Judy should have donned Mum's mantle and became the matriarch. But that's not what happened. Until my mother's death at age ninety-eight, the natural order, as usual, was thrown into chaos.

———

My mother and Judy were the voices, the truths, deep inside me. They were the storytellers, the cheerleaders, the ones who believed in me: my mother, whose heart could stop at any moment, and finally did, and my sister Judy, who in the year before her death wasn't telling us the extent of her troubles. For them I would do anything. The job I set myself after their deaths isn't just to tell their stories, but to recompose the harmony of our days. I have written this as my sister died, as my mother lived six more years, and when she, too, died. This story is my attempt at restoration.

———

A bald eagle drifts and turns, watching us, catching the currents of the mountain air, the river, and the heat of the spring sun. Brier rolls in long, golden grasses below the cottonwood, and her coat is sweet with the scent of their catkins.

Pin Curls Rule: 2010

Two Years Earlier

I once wrote fiery speeches and delivered them on the street, on International Women's Day or the anniversary of the Montreal Massacre. Now I put my mother's hair up in pin curls.

My mother and I wait in her hospital room. We wait for the doctors to decide, finally, if they will do the experimental surgery that could save her life. I'm about to learn that pin curls have as much power as well-crafted speeches.

My mother, Edna Mae Moir, better known as Erin, is ninety-one years old. She has inspired some people, women in particular, because she said to me, a young reporter who had offended a powerful person, "Honey, if you're not on somebody's shit list, you're no damned good."

Women in trouble at work or home or out on the hustings tell me that her analysis and spirit, her pride in my being on someone's shit list, gave them strength when they needed it most. That's who she is in my world, in British Columbia, where people don't know my mother personally, but have read or heard her words because I am a reporter and writer.

Our family is far-flung across Canada and the US. I am a "Canadian born abroad," born in the US in 1952 with Canadian citizenship. I have lived all over Canada since I was fourteen, and in rural British Columbia since I was twenty-three, now with my partner, Dan.

My family history sounds complex, but it's only because our father was a botanist, an explorer on Hudson Bay, whose drive for an education and work in his field took our family back and forth across the Canada/US border, where my mother bore five of us in three different hospitals, and where our nationalities and cross-border moves became somewhat confusing.

My two brothers, Brian and Andy, were born in Canada and live in Winnipeg and Nova Scotia; my sister Judy, the oldest, was born in Canada and became a US citizen. I was born in the US with Canadian citizenship, as was my sister Donna, who then became a US citizen. My parents became US citizens and except for another stint in Canada in the 1960s, lived in the US the rest of their lives. While my brothers and I and many of our relatives live in Canada, my mother, sisters, nephew, nieces and extended family live in the US. The cross-border and far-flung location of our family homes mean that for decades I have driven vast distances, especially in my early years, from my rural world in BC to urban centres—Winnipeg and St. Paul—to small villages such as my brother's in Nova Scotia, and back again.

When I think of our father's long-distance explorations,

and subsequently my own, I think of our family as a pack that separated to the farthest points of our northern world, each needing that much territory to roam in and establish our dens, to pitch our own tents.

I live in a rural valley in the mountains; my mother lives in urban St. Paul, where she's made her home for about forty years. She lives in a carriage house, the building where carriages once pulled by horses were stored. Long ago carriage houses were converted into homes along the old brick-lined alleyways in her part of St. Paul. She lives behind my sister Judy's home on Summit Avenue, a historic boulevard lined with big trees and mansions a century old. Judy's is a three-storey home built in 1901, and two floors are dedicated to her (and now her son's) wedding catering business.

Judy and Mum each live alone, side by side. Judy is sixty-five, and has scleroderma, a serious heart and lung condition. Mum is ninety-one, alert, smart and charming, but exhausted. The central valve in her heart is stenotic, narrowed, almost closed. Where once we talked politics and the issues of the day, now she mostly bends forward and says, "I can't breathe. I'm drowning." It's time for me, far away in British Columbia, to help out, to make the trek of 2,500 km between my mountain home and my family's home in Minnesota.

⎯

In the midst of my concern for my mother and her worsening heart condition, I am worried about Judy, who along with my sister Donna has been taking care of Mum. Judy lives a few steps across the backyard and is Mum's mainstay.

When I phoned Judy to say I could come help, she reacted in her big sister way. "No, we're fine. Let's just wait a bit. Let's see what the doctors have to say." Judy will accept help when she needs it, but it is hard for her to ask. She has always taken care of us, has worn the mantel of big sisterhood as a comfortable cloak and we have benefited from her reassurances, her solid footing as the oldest sibling.

I think of our family as holding down the pegs of a giant circus tent that stretches from BC to Winnipeg and Nova Scotia and down to Minnesota. Judy is the centre pole of our family tent. Mum and Dad steadied it as Judy grew stronger through all our family crises. Then Dad died, and now Mum's ascendance is waning. The main support of a circus tent is called the King Pole, but in our family we have a Queen Pole: Judy.

Judy is dark-haired, brown-eyed and olive-skinned. She could have been from the Mediterranean, or a dark Scot like our father. Her eyes are acute and piercing like his sometimes, other times scrunched up with laughter. She is five feet three inches tall and petite, though once she was heavy. She lost weight after her husband, Michael, died and her sons, David and William, went off to university. Then William died. She stopped eating so much red meat, the fuel of men, and turned more to salads and fish, small portions, the sustenance of a woman living on her own.

I am light-haired, blue-eyed and freckled. I could be from Ireland, like our mother's people. Of the five siblings, two are dark, three light, yet we all look alike. Judy was the first born, then Brian (blue-eyed), Andy (brown-eyed), me (blue), and Donna (blue). None of us has had any cosmetic surgery done on our faces; none of us had braces; all of us have the same distinctive canine teeth. We each have varied in our lives from fat to thin and back again. All of us have smoked, and then all but one stopped.

Judy and I were far enough apart in age—seven years— that we didn't know each other well as we grew up, never even attended the same school together; but we have grown close as adults. We have weathered and laughed our way through our adult lives, through the tragic and the ludicrous.

So I know my sister well enough that I don't believe her when she protests that she and Mum are doing fine. She protests that it's too far for me to come. She protests that it will take me from my work.

"You need a rest," I finally say. "I'm leaving on Monday."

"Okay," she concedes, after more back and forth of this nature. "If you're sure."

"I'm sure. I've got everything ready."

"Okay then. Drive safely," she says. While I've often driven the three days to get there, this time I will fly, but she knows even the four-hour drive to the plane in Spokane can be treacherous in winter. "It will be good to have you here. We'll have some fun, too. Everyone will be glad to see you."

By everyone she means our large extended family, and her group of close friends who I've come to know over the decades.

Before we hang up she asks: "What are you drinking, red or white?"

"Anything."

———

I know my mother suffers severe heart problems, but I am unaware of how serious Judy's own heart and lung issues are. Talking to each of them, I glean this picture: every night they don overcoats and boots and Judy helps Mum along the snowed-in icy paths of Judy's backyard, because Mum can't spend the nights alone, and Judy, allergic to Mum's cat, can't stay with her. The short path between the two houses is treacherous: Mum stops to breathe and rest. Judy's lungs and heart strain in the frigid cold and with each brief pause, poor circulation causes further pain in her already swollen feet. They make this trek in the dark, across the yard, up to the second floor where each tiny woman crawls into Judy's king-sized bed, Judy helping Mum up the small stepladder onto the giant mattress.

I travel to St. Paul because I know my sister's voice. I know when she is hiding exhaustion; I have some sixth sense with her that even though she is my older sister, even though she is magnificent and capable, there are times when she needs help but won't ask for it. When it is my help, specifically, that she needs. I know she doesn't want to interrupt my writing, or pull me so many miles down from my own snowed-in mountain home to hers on the prairies. My sister is battling her own disease and doesn't want us to know the toll it takes.

But when she picks me up at the airport, it's clear I made the right choice. Judy is haggard; there is none of her ready laughter and our drive to her house is full of details of what lies ahead.

Judy warns me that Mum is very weak. We know that only the replacement of her aortic valve will save her life; it will be the second attempt to replace it.

⸺

Usually the valve is replaced, routinely and successfully, by the traditional method where they open the chest. Two years earlier a medical team had tried this, but partway through, the head surgeon had emerged from the operating theatre where our mother lay cracked open like a lobster, to tell us she had a "porcelain" aorta. Her aorta was heavily calcified; it was brittle and fragile and couldn't withstand the stress of the operation. She would likely die if the porcelain-like shards broke loose. Even as he explained the danger, I was struck by the beauty of the language, how lethal a beautiful image could become: porcelain, like old fine china, which could shatter, as if dropped from a shelf. It would move through her like small splinters, he said, and she could have a stroke and die. He would not proceed. After that failed surgery two years ago, they stapled her up and wheeled her out of the operating room. The doctor consoled us that maybe someday, in Minnesota as they were doing in Vancouver (and he had said this with a nod to the Canadians in the family), they could put in a new valve without opening her chest. He explained that the valve could be pushed through the femoral artery up into the heart. Maybe someday in a few years. They're doing experiments, he had said. They would stay in touch.

Someday over the rainbow, we thought back then as we looked at our feet and shuffled out of the hospital, carrying that slim hope along with the heart pillow and the varicosity socks. Mum went into transitional care, an old folks' home where for weeks she recovered from sawed-open ribs over the same old unfixed heart. Then she'd waited for her valve to close, and thus her death.

———

Our over-the-rainbow day has come, though. Surgery is set up at the Mayo Clinic, in Rochester, Minnesota. She is the oldest person in human trials by a major drug company.

The entire family will be with Mum for this experimental surgery.

Andy and Brian will travel from Nova Scotia and Manitoba. My sisters, Judy and Donna, Judy's son David and his wife, Amber, and all the extended family, will help her through this.

We will do everything: hold her, wheel her, chide her; we will bring together all our organizational and emotional strengths. We will sing and play music for her, cook for her, tell her she better not die; that she has one last shot if the doctors, with all their tests and their new technology, can just get inside her and put in the spare part.

Then as we drive along snowy Summit Avenue, Judy tells me, almost as an aside, that she, too, has some surgery coming up and she's waiting for a date: they're going to insert a catheter that delivers medicine into a vein that enters her heart; it's not a big operation, she says, it's not booked yet, and compared to Mum's it will be a walk in the park.

When Judy pulls into her driveway and drops me at my parents', Mum is so happy to see me—a big hug and bigger smile, her blue eyes brimming with gladness that another one of "her kids" is with her, shrewd with the knowledge that I may have made it just in time. She's on her chesterfield with her cat beside her, surrounded by books and plants and lamps. She's in her element, her home, safe and secure even in this crisis. She's lived here almost forty years, in this home where carriages and horses were stabled a century ago; where the walls are still the lovely old glazed brick; where Dad, a carpenter and woodworker, has created the Irish cottage my mother always wanted. The floors are beautiful old tongue-and-groove fir, the many-paned windows are divided with real wood, not vinyl. Mum has decorated with lace curtains from Ireland and braided rugs; tapes and CDs of Irish music and books about Ireland are everywhere. She's painted one wall a bright glowing orange, not what you'd call Irish, really, but she loves the daring splash that startles and causes comment.

"Sorry it's such a mess," she says. "I just haven't been up to much cleaning."

The house is charming, but the charm has been fading these last years; except for the splash of orange, it has grown claustrophobic, with too many decorative plates furred with dust on high shelves, old coats and photo albums crammed in closets, worn-out cosmetics crowding the bathroom sink, too many drawers stuffed with stuff.

"Rita, open the door," Judy calls from the entryway through the garage. "Thought we needed a treat."

So there's Judy, exhausted and beat, but she's rallied herself, and she knows she will rally us, with some nourishment. This is her signal to me that "we're on," and we're going to stay on until we're done.

"You're a good kid," Mum says, and samples pieces of what Judy knows are her favourites, prawns and shrimp sauce, cheese and sourdough, and treats left from her last catering job.

⎯

That first night, I slept on Mum's living room chesterfield right below her bedroom.

She'd agreed reluctantly to pound on the floor above my head with her cane if she needed help. But, exhausted, I slept through her pounding and calls, and she made her way downstairs to the bathroom alone. When Mum made coffee and told me, I felt sheepish; the relief staff who blows the first shift. Mum thought it proved she could do fine alone. But we all know that's not true anymore, so the three of us explored the options—an emergency lifeline that Mum could press to alert some person in a far-off place who would then turn around and call me on Mum's telephone a floor below. It all seemed stupid and expensive and would take too long to set into action.

Then a friend suggested we buy a cheap and very loud battery-operated doorbell that Mum could operate from her bed. Ludicrously buoyed by the simplicity of the solution and the task, Judy and I jumped in her van and set off for the hardware store.

I fiddled with the many options for the ring tone: the simple, traditional ding dong; "The Star Spangled Banner" ("the rocket's red glare, the bombs bursting in air"); "Cotton Fields Back Home."

Upstairs, Mum pushed the doorbell button, which nestled in her house robe pocket; the doorbell, placed on a stool next to my sleeping head, was set loud enough to wake the dead. John Philip Sousa's "Stars and Stripes Forever" (Be Kind to Your Web-Footed Friends) blasted me into consciousness. I was in the US, ready to march.

———

Last week's snowy mountain roads and the airplane's sweeping vista of prairie are far behind me now. I have entered the claustrophobia and minutiae of caregiving: the doorbell is repeatedly lost, found and retrieved; the days are full of canes and keys, laundry, naps, visits to the doctor, cleaning cluttered surfaces and picking up bobby pins, the artifacts of a woman of a certain age.

My mother drips bobby pins. They hide in corners of the bathroom floor, embed themselves in the braided carpet in the living room that is crowded with rocking chairs and end tables. Bobby pins await me on chiffoniers, they sequester themselves in sweater pockets headed for the washer, cling to the terrycloth that Mum twists around her bobby-pinned hair.

When she puts that towel turban on, she looks like a movie star from the 1950s, Greta Garbo or Katharine Hepburn. My mother, now so tiny, has good bones, has lost all the Irish porridge fat that she, at age forty-two, complained to her own mother about.

She once wore wigs, in the days when she owned several Merle Norman Cosmetics studios. Her hair is fine, takes a curl nicely, but how fun it was instead to clap on a wig, be a blonde Monday, redhead through the workweek, brunette Friday night. What fun to choose different clothes and makeup, do a makeover.

Now Mum applies a bit of lipstick, combs out the pin curls and that's it. She really doesn't need more, because her eyes are blue, and her frame so slender she can put on an old pair of black stretch pants, loose and hanging, a black turtleneck, maybe a scarf, and her eyes and cheekbones take over. She's down to 119 pounds, 5 foot 3. About a size 8.

Sometimes Mum asked, "Will you put my hair up?" or "Will you comb it out for me?" and though she'd done it so many times for us when we were children with heads full of bobby pins, we'd never done it for her. We worked with our fumbling hands; Judy's fingers cold and swollen with Raynaud's disease, my hands more accustomed to gripping a chainsaw. We wet the comb, or dipped our fingers in warm water before winding strands of her thinning hair in little loops and fastening them against her scalp. We could barely manage, with hair escaping our clumsy fingers, bobby pins crisscrossed at odd angles, her head a thatch of metal that must have made sleeping unpleasant. But it made her happy, so we were happy. The next morning she smiled as she leaned back, as we carefully removed the bobby pins, lightly combed out each curl and then styled it as best we could, because it made her feel better, because she had grown so weak, her heart so strained, that she couldn't hold her hands above her head long enough to do this simple task of grooming.

In those intimate days, this was my favourite image: Mum all in black, sitting, elegant in her slenderness, hair Daryl Hannah-like, wet and shaggy-dog; Judy so tiny, standing behind her in a black and white patterned jacket and black pants; both awaiting their surgeries, Judy setting Mum's pin curls and both of them laughing, even as they recalled our losses, Judy's son William who died in 2002 and Dad in 2003.

Judy remembers Dad asking repeatedly: "William, how does the Internet work?"

I can see Dad and William: Dad old, white-haired and craggy, in the green sweater he always wore along with his battered fishing hat, sitting in his worn leather chair. William, young, handsome and headstrong and just beginning to understand the art of patience, especially with Dad, who was often confused and forgetful.

William would stand before him, brow furrowed, gesturing with his hands to explain the Internet, perhaps in technical terms that Dad might normally comprehend, but with Alzheimer's he couldn't understand or couldn't remember, so later he'd say, "Judy, explain that to me again. How does the signal get to the computer? Who runs the Internet?"

Judy, gesturing with comb and bobby pins in hand, says to Mum: "I'd say: 'You know, Dad? It's a mystery. The Internet just works, that's all.'"

As she finishes pinning up Mum's hair, she muses, in one of the very few references I ever heard her make to an afterlife, "Well, maybe Dad and William have met up somewhere, and William's still trying to explain."

⸺

Despite all evidence to the contrary, I do not think I will lose my mother and sister, or at least I won't let my mind go there. In my family we fix things. The furniture is broken, you repair it. The truck is old; carry extra oil and brake fluid. We are not stupid; we understand realities, we are deeply schooled in accidents and sudden death, but in the normal course of things, just as with our dogs, who all live past their expected lifespans, we, too, outlive anyone's expectations. Don't tell us a golden retriever only lives to twelve. Ours live to fourteen or eighteen. Our nana lived to ninety-six, our father to eighty-three; our mother is ninety-one. In our family we operate on the basis, as counterpoint to early and tragic death, that with willpower and good care we'll march along a bit longer. There's a problem? Fix it and keep on moving.

—

Judy and I set up an electronic talking scale delivered by Mum's health care provider; through the phone line it transmits Mum's weight and her answers to a distant "heart failure" nurse, who must be as confused by my mother's answers as Mum is by the rapid-fire questions. (Are you watching your sodium intake? asks the monotone and robotic voice. *Yes!* Mum answers, glaring at the monitor. Are you more tired today? *If I were more tired I'd be dead*, my mother snaps back at the yes or no option. Are you taking your medication?) The nurse at the end of the phone line somewhere charts weight gains of more than a few pounds in a day or five pounds in a week, a warning sign of fluid retention.

I spend nights with Mum, and Judy arrives early to help with the morning regimen: get up, go to the bathroom. Rest. Put on slip and housecoat. Rest. Take off housecoat. Stand on scale, hands must be at sides. Press start button. When it's over, back on with the housecoat. Rest. Then coffee. Pills before food. Pills after food. Shower, get dressed, breakfast; the routine takes two hours.

Mum grows weaker, seriously weaker. Her weight drops rapidly for someone already so small. She loses ten pounds in three weeks. She can't eat, or eats so little.

The date for surgery is not flexible, so we are doing all we can to keep Mum alive until then.

We pull out all the tricks: Judy a professional caterer, and me who simply loves cooking. We serve food in small Japanese bowls, black lacquer with gold symbols, or on the bright orange plates Mum's found at rummage sales. We create dainty arrangements with slices of orange and melon amidst triangles of toast, or pickled ginger beside three delicate salmon sushi. Like artists, we arrange tomato wedges and cucumber sticks, tiny tastes of barbequed pork, balsamic vinegar and olive oil on small green salads.

"I can't eat," she'd say.

"You have to eat," we'd say. "Just try a bit. Just three bites."

⎯

Judy looks better. She's had time to rest and reconnect with friends, even to play Mahjong with them. We are on more equal footing now, she a bit more rested, me a bit more tired.

While we spend much of each day with Mum, Judy also slips away for her own medical appointments. Sometimes her son David, or his wife, Amber, who is a nurse, go with her. Like Mum, Judy is on Lasix and many other drugs to relieve fluid retention and thus ease the pressure on her heart and lungs.

If Mum struggled to breathe, Judy could look at her with understanding and say truthfully, "Yes, I know. It sucks. But we just have to keep on going."

——

Scleroderma: the term derma makes it sound like a skin condition but it can affect the lungs and heart and other organs. In the past year Judy had sent us emails outlining her condition, so she hadn't kept us out of the loop, but each one ended optimistically. She had a great medical team, she was feeling better, they had a new technique or a new drug to try out.

We should have known how serious this was, but we really didn't. We were all concentrating on Mum, whose condition was so visibly obvious and nearing crisis. And Judy was too high functioning, too omnipotent. I feel compelled to say she wasn't a saint, so she doesn't seem too good to be real, but in this way she was. She put Mum first. She did not slyly make sure we knew how serious her own problems were so she could play the martyr. She put Mum first and that was it. In the shadow of Mum's situation, we all failed to understand what was going on. We made lists and we checked off jobs accomplished; in that list making and our accomplishments, we found our stride.

And Judy was a master at making lists and hiding her troubles beneath them.

——

We do fun things, as she promised. Mum is still able to spend a few hours alone at home, so Judy and I drive on snowy roads out to a suburban theatre to watch a live Metropolitan Opera broadcast of *Carmen*. We nestle in next to each other and glory in the beat and life of the familiar aria: *Toréador, L'Amour t'attend. Toreador, Love awaits you!* The costumes, the music, the very over-the-top opera-ness of it, make everything seem bigger, fuller, more lush, as if in comparison our dilemmas and hardships are both insignificant and worthy of huge arias themselves.

The next day, on my fifty-eighth birthday, Judy makes a special brunch for Mum and me and Donna's family. Later Judy and all her friends treat me to calamari and wine at a downtown restaurant. It's going to be a gruelling week ahead before surgery, and we do our best to remain upbeat, like cheerleaders preparing for the big game. From my birthday on, we don't leave Mum alone for a minute. We are as close to full-time care as you could find outside a hospital.

———

Judy and I braced Mum between us to help her shuffle through the living room to the bathroom. Mum panicked, gasping for air, drowning in her own fluids.

"Mum, Mum, sit for minute," we said as we tried to calm her, fighting back our own tears. We were terrified by our two options: if we called the ambulance, the Mayo Clinic would find out and conclude she was too weak for the operation. But if we didn't get help immediately, she could die.

Our slight hold on control was beginning to disintegrate. That week Judy had received the call for her own heart surgery.

"I know the timing isn't great," she said, in what later could be considered a classic understatement. "But I've been waiting for a while. I better get this done. Can you manage?"

"Yes," I'd said. "Of course." I was so sure I could manage, that I would manage, that for Judy to admit she needed this must mean she really needed it. Taking care of Mum was the support I could offer to Judy, so that she, too, could get better.

As we held Mum upright, one of us on each side of her, I looked across Mum's shoulders into Judy's eyes: "Should we call the ambulance?"

"I think maybe," Judy said.

"No, wait, I'll be okay," Mum insisted as her breathing eased. That night, she slept sitting up on the couch with me nearby. The next morning we sat tight. If we didn't make any sudden moves, we could perhaps manage.

Judy's stepson Terry, a doctor, dropped by, looked at Mum and ran back out to his car through the deep snowbanks for his stethoscope.

"Think of it as going in for a tune-up," he said to Mum. "You're too crackly. Too much fluid in your lungs. They'll tune you up for Mayo." He had her admitted to nearby United Hospital immediately, where David's wife, Amber, worked.

"How's everything going?" Amber asked with her beautiful big North Dakota smile, as she walked into Mum's room and checked her charts and fluids. As Mum took Amber's hand, I could sense her security in Amber's presence, was so relieved at her young competence, her confidence even in the face of our difficult reality. And I felt that shift that happens when things come back together, as if all the support structures, all the guardian angels, are flying in formation.

At this hospital on one side of the Mississippi River in St. Paul, I stayed with Mum while David and Amber drove Judy across the bridge for her surgery on the other side, at a hospital in Minneapolis. So very odd that that they were in hospitals at the same time, across the river from each other, both with hearts about to be opened, as if the river itself were some symbol of separation, of connection.

Surgeons inserted a Hickman catheter into a vein that entered Judy's enlarged and overworked heart. For the rest of her too short life she would be attached to a small pump that pulsed and whirred, delivering into her a medical broth called Remodulin.

With my mother and sister secure in their separate hospitals, I slept in my room on the third floor at Judy's house, getting a true rest with no emergency doorbell jangling me awake, no burden of care or worry to jar me from sleep. Those nights it was strange to walk the creaky halls, alone upstairs in Judy's old mansion, with no human or animal to keep me company. Once a hub of family life, the third floor was now a repository of old bedsprings, worn-out microwaves, a snooker table covered in a dusty green tarp. The only life was the one remaining fish, a languid black *Plecostomus*, hiding amidst the plastic arch and fronds of its large tank.

"You must be hungry," I said aloud, and pinched out a good helping of fish flakes.

The next day the phone rang in Mum's hospital room and it was Judy, post-surgery, calling from her own hospital bed: she and Mum compared menus. I watched Mum as I heard Judy's laughter through the phone line, watched Mum's face light up.

Those were the lovely moments: who ordered the stir-fries (low sodium), who ordered chicken (no skin).

But in another sense, I was in charge, and I wasn't used to being in charge. I was normally the very reliable second-in-command, with older sister Judy in charge. Or when the whole family was together, we were all in charge. I am excellent at making arrangements, carrying out tasks, initiating and researching, at thinking and speaking eloquently and frankly; but when it came to giving the final nod, in our family we looked to Judy, who would also look to Mum. My two matriarchs were missing in action, so there I was negotiating parking ramps and city traffic, even doing the simple things like using house keys and never leaving keys in a car, all those chores that in a city are normal, but for someone from the country, where we leave our keys in the car and never lock the house, well, I had to think every step of the way. Make post-it notes to myself. Don't lock the keys in the car. Don't hit the panic button.

On the other hand, in my own element, I'm damned handy with a chainsaw.

The doctor attending Mum warned me that while intravenous diuretics would provide temporary relief, eventually they'd cause liver damage. He seemed sceptical about the upcoming valve replacement surgery at the Mayo Clinic, and made it clear I shouldn't be hopeful. He cautioned me to inform them of this admission and treatment. I truthfully hoped I wouldn't have to, that maybe we could waltz Mum down to the Mayo Clinic looking like a million bucks and they'd never be the wiser. All I wanted was to get Mum home, whisper a triumphant "Ally, Ally in Free," and with Andy and Brian arriving from Canada, Judy home, and a weekend of rest, we'd all head the eighty miles to Rochester, to the Mayo Clinic for Mum's final tests and surgery.

Instead, I bundled Mum home from the hospital and with trepidation, dutifully left a message for Betty Anderson, co-ordinator of the Mayo surgical team, who warned the head surgeon, who wanted to reassess Mum immediately, the next day. Weeks of extensive testing in November and December preceded her selection for this operation. Our worst fear, despite Mum's tune-up, was that by hospitalizing her, we had jeopardized everything.

Andy and Brian hadn't arrived, and I had to get Mum to Rochester first thing in the morning, a place I'd never been, and who knew if we were coming back? Literally. Mum could die in surgery (if they did surgery), or even before surgery, and this could be her last night in her home. I could not get emotional; I simply had to take control.

Though I aimed for calm and serenity, that night was bedlam. I ran back and forth on the icy sidewalks between Judy's and Mum's gathering dirty laundry from my third-floor room, made supper for Mum and me, fielded calls between Judy in the hospital and Andy and Brian en route as I scrambled to change plans. Woke Andy up in his Halifax airport hotel room, tracked Brian down on the treacherous winter roads from Winnipeg. Medical records had to be faxed to Mayo, a million notes written to those who would arrive after we left early in the morning. I am grim and determined and scared.

Mum is bummed out and flustered as I race around.

I'm yelling at her, asking her what she wants me to pack.

When you always yell at a person, because they can't hear and there isn't a hearing aid made that will work properly, you end up feeling uptight and angry. It's not normal to always yell, or to project your voice so much you feel like you're yelling.

"What clothes do you want?" I holler. Upstairs, though her bedroom now is in complete disorder—she hasn't been strong enough for months to put her clothes away properly—she still knows where everything is, or should be.

"The yellow top," she says. "And those brown velour pants. No, I think I wore those yesterday."

"They're in the wash!" I yell. "They're warm! They look good on you!"

My mum watches me scramble, and it's hard for her. Hard for both of us, because of the unspoken: this isn't calm; it's chaotic. We're not all here laughing and finding our collective strength; everyone's everywhere, scattered. She hates calling on me, on all of us, for all this help. She hates having to ring a wireless doorbell at night that rings next to my head so I can roll off the couch and be with her when she comes down to the bathroom. She hates all this.

"I'm sitting here completely useless," she says. "I used to be able to do this for myself." I know this; I sympathize, but in this moment and for this once, I can't handle this mantra. I am too tired, too anxious, trying too hard to make it all go right, and with an armload of laundry, I turn on her.

"Mum, you are going to Mayo. You are going to get a new heart valve on Tuesday. I will personally give you artificial respiration all the way there if I have to. But I can't do this without you tonight. I need you to be positive as much as you need me." I am yelling (of course), almost sobbing. "Now where's your fighting spirit!"

"Give me those clothes," she orders, "at least I can sort the damned socks." I dump the bundle on her lap, and the absurdity of it sets us off, both of us laughing and back in gear. "Thanks for saying that, honey," she says, slamming the white socks into little balls. And then Judy calls from a hospital phone, co-ordinating everything as fast as she can from her end. Her stepdaughter Cass is there and will come help. David will pick us up in the morning, so I don't have to drive a cold Minnesota highway, with our sick mother, on roads I don't know to a place I've never been.

Cass arrives with a relaxation tape, something we would normally never consider, let alone use. But it is so right tonight, a soothing video of Japanese gardens that Mum once visited. To the soothing Japanese music, and a soothing narration, Cass brushes Mum's hair and massages her head and temples and back, does some warm-hand-healing-touch things like reiki, Cass-kinds-of-things that in this moment relax Mum and let me pack, clean and phone. I plaster post-it notes all over the kitchen cupboards and on the doors. Some to remind me of each step I need to take: "Put the key on Judy's table." "Lock the door." "Leave the garage light on." I quiet myself with lists: phone lists with everyone's cell and home phone numbers for Brian and Andy, who will arrive to both Judy's and Mum's empty houses in the dark. I tape up a list of the food I just bought: "Andy, there's meatloaf in the fridge." "Brian, there's canned salmon in the pantry and fresh salad stuff in the crisper."

Mum and I are ready by 7:30 the next morning, sitting like two old Prairie ladies with our suitcases on our laps two hours before the trip. We are packed, showered, weighed in and dressed; we are fed, pills have been taken, boots zippered, cane found; the keys are in her purse, the call has been made to the cardiologist's office to have records sent, and we're waiting for word from Mayo about the appointment time. The cat is fed and licking her paws; we are smiling, clutching our gloves and keeping everything positive: "We're ready, Mum. We're on the way for your new valve!"

At 8 a.m., the surgical team co-ordinator calls: she can get us in at 11:30. David arrives with his big warm SUV to pick us up. Calm, wonderful David in a big warm car, to help frail little Mum over the snowbank, and me with the valises of clothes, the big anti-bedsore cushion and, thank god, a few bottles of wine.

——

The heart surgeon looked grim as he left the examining room to consult with a cardiologist, and we sat with our hearts in our throats.

"We'll admit you and then we'll see," he said to Mum.

——

I settled into the motel room Judy booked for us across from the hospital. Such a Judy thing: to book the right place, to put the bill in her name, even to reassure me that she would cover the costs. All this accomplished from her own hospital bed and knowing my financial resources were already strained from the long trip. Brian helped Andy that way, too, because Andy had to travel so far and the costs are huge. Donna and her family will all arrive soon and be across the hall; David and Amber will arrive and our strength will carry us through whatever lies ahead.

——

That first night at the Mayo Clinic, when Mum asks me to put her hair up in pin curls, we are alone. She passes me bobby pins, grinning at my attempts, when the surgeon walks in to examine her again. We both know that for all her bravado, he had been looking at a sick woman earlier in the day, and he's going to keep a very close watch.

"I'll see you on morning rounds," he says, after listening to her heart and making entries on the computer.

"What time?" I ask.

———

I'm there by 6:30. Wake Mum. She feels better after a night of professional care and prepares to ace this morning exam: out of bed, teeth brushed, in her housecoat, sitting up in her reclining chair, ready for me to remove the bobby pins and brush her hair out in waves. Lipstick on, eyes shining, Irish charm in gear.

The surgeon arrives with three colleagues. He's a personable man, professional. He relaxes. He checks her charts on the computer, takes some vitals. He reviews the situation for us and for his colleagues: reminds us that she is the oldest person in the trial. Rather than open her chest to gain access to the aortic valve, they will open her femoral artery and, internally, slide the new valve up to her heart. If she survives the operation, she should recover far more quickly than with the traditional procedure.

"How are you feeling?" he asks.

"Like a million bucks and even better when you put in that valve," she says, blue eyes twinkling and shrewd.

"I'm happier about how you're looking," he says.

"What does that mean?" I ask. (I *am* curious—what do they look for? Skin colour? Brightness of eye? Snappy comebacks?)

"Just clinically, her appearance," he says, looking at me. "I saw her yesterday in my office for the first time since December" (and he doesn't have to say he was shocked, if not downright alarmed), and then he turns to Mum, "but last night I saw you sitting up getting your hair done, and today you're smiling. There is absolutely no doubt now that we will go ahead with surgery."

I can't help it; tears are spilling out of my eyes. Mum and I look at each other.

Pin curls rule.

⸺

Mum's ensconced in her room, charming nurses and orderlies, so I get out to explore: "Saint Marys Hospital" says the sign on the building where we enter the Mayo complex. Why no possessive apostrophe in Saint Marys, I had to ask, as if I, the writer, might inform them there is a typo in all their publicity and on the front of their building.

I noticed this odd spelling after being awed by the stained glass, the heavy front doors made with brass handles and elegant metal grids (my partner, Dan, who is a blacksmith, would love this) and the paintings of the nuns, which adorn the labyrinth of corridors I always get lost in without my more geographically savvy siblings at my side.

"Because the possessive makes it like Saint Mary owns it, and it's really everyone's," says the woman postering the halls for the nuns' rummage sale. This lack of apostrophe still makes no sense to me, but then, it's not my story.

She tells me the rummage sale raises funds for people who can't pay for treatment. She explains that Saint Marys is one part of the Mayo Clinic and, oddly, it is in the practical nature of this conversation that it truly dawns on me that I am standing inside the famed Mayo Clinic, a name I've known since I was a child. That our mother will receive treatment here.

As I stand before her in this place that fills me with awe, part of my mind fetches a childhood memory of the dreaded Mayo Clinic Diet, a horrid regime of boiled eggs, overcooked spinach and grapefruit, from when Mum and I dieted endlessly. Awful, awful canned spinach.

But I jerk back into the present, because even as a child I always knew the Mayo Clinic was revered throughout the world. The Mayo Clinic, the best, where the treatment was the most thorough: at the Mayo Clinic, they wouldn't give up if a sensible solution were to be found. I always knew that if there were a place, anywhere, to inspire confidence and hope, it was the Mayo Clinic.

The woman before me, putting up posters, would soon inspire us with her own hope and confidence.

⸺

Andy and Brian arrive from Canada. Judy, with her new heart catheter and pump, is released from hospital and back in the driver's seat, figuratively and literally. This is my big sister: she may be weak, she may not have much stamina post-surgery, but nothing on god's green earth would keep her from being with Mum for her operation.

On Saturday she and my brothers talk and laugh the whole way from St. Paul to meet us at the Mayo Clinic. I swear the bunch of them light up the hallways. They tease me about all the post-it notes I plastered all over Mum's house to greet them, thank me for the food I'd prepared for their arrival; and then I relax into having three older siblings who can take over for a while.

Mum never was aware that Judy was too weak to walk any distance and for the whole time used a wheelchair. But each time we approached Mum's room, Judy rose from the wheelchair and strode in smiling. She was adamant that Mum spend none of her energy worrying about her. And through all the pre-surgery days, as some of us stayed with Mum, Judy and Brian drove back and forth the eighty miles to St. Paul for Judy's post-surgical checks for infection of the heart catheter, checks on the mixture of Remodulin.

A friend had asked by email, "Where are your brothers in all of this? Is it always the sisters who do the caregiving?" It's a valid question, of course, and one that some decades ago I may have answered differently. But this time, I could write back and say, our brothers are here and they are full of laughter and care, and they will cook and wash dishes and carry Mum in their arms if that is what she needs. Our brothers have arrived, and it's like having more angels at our wings.

———

At the Mayo Clinic, though half our family lives in the US, we soon became known as "The Canadians." We were an oddity, neighbours but slightly exotic; from The North, a place people may have travelled to but didn't really understand. Obama's Medicare bill was on everyone's minds, so staff and strangers asked us questions about Medicare or simply about Canada. Several of the Mayo staff were Canadian, or had Canadian relatives. They sought us out; the cardiologist from Nova Scotia talked to Andy about fish, Betty the co-ordinator had kids in Montreal, another doctor had relatives in Vancouver and Calgary, the anaesthesiologist long ago lived in Manitoba. There wasn't a day when someone didn't say, "Oh, the Canadians," in recognition of our family as we sat in waiting rooms or roved the corridors. And we, in humble Canadian deference, would acknowledge that some of our family are Minnesotans. After all, it was their state and their amazing hospital we were visiting, and where all of us, regardless of nationality, were welcomed like long-lost family.

———

Andy was worn out, but so present and accounted for. All that winter in their home in Nova Scotia, Andy and his wife, Chris, had cared round the clock for Chris's elderly parents. Following a good meal and the pleasure of hearing Andy pound out the much-loved "Battle Hymn of the Republic," Chris's father had died.

It was soon after his funeral that Andy drove from his fishing village, Freeport, to Halifax, to fly to Minnesota to help with Mum.

Andy and I stayed together in the motel. As teenagers we were close, even sang together publicly, but this time we were not teenagers, or even young adults, but older adults. And I watched my exhausted brother muster all his strength and reserve.

⎯

I buy flowers to brighten Mum's room, rub her back and feet, find brochures about the hospital and its history and the art-work, but I don't think of getting a wheelchair and giving Mum a tour. Andy does because he'd been wheeling Chris's father around all winter.

Mum is so happy to have her kids with her—all five of us. She's looking so good, so ready for anything. Sure, she's suffering heart failure, she's thin and worn out; sure, she could die on the operating table, but her kids are gathering and she's in one of the world's best hospitals getting the best possible care.

"Wanna go for a spin?" Andy asks.

"You betcha!" she says, and the nurse bundles her in blankets and disconnects cords and gear.

"Would you like a concert?" Andy asks as he wheels Mum to the grand piano in the foyer. On a Sunday morning in a

Catholic hospital, he hammers out a boogie-woogie and then as if we were teenagers again, we sing "House of the Rising Sun" and "Somewhere over the Rainbow."

As Andy plays, with Mum's wheelchair close to the piano, people brusque with cold push in through the huge metal doors, slow their pace, then pause to listen. They slip quietly onto small benches along the wall, underneath the stained glass. Andy moves from song to song; sometimes I sing a few lines, accustomed to standing by him singing as we did when we were young.

People watch Mum, I think even envy her, and later in the corridors of the hospital, they stop Andy to tell him how much his music helped them that morning.

A man asks if we've been to the chapel. We figure, why not, and after we admire a multi-faith meditation room, head down to the Catholic quarter.

My mother is not a Catholic. Her own mother rejected the church, effectively ending generations' worth of Catholicism in our lineage. In our family, a chapel is no longer a religious experience, but an admiration of architecture, a love of silence or music, even grandeur.

Mum is old Irish, and political: the sins of the Catholic Church are not lost on her: the abuse, the opulence. At first in this beautiful chapel, she sees only the waste of money; what could have been used to help the poor has gone instead into carved sandstone, walls of green marble, pillars of pearl white granite.

But in the quiet, two days before her own surgery and maybe her death, she puts all that aside.

"It's very beautiful, isn't it?" she admits, "in spite of everything," giving the Church, for this moment, her own absolution.

She wants to get closer to the altar, and briefly stands so she can touch the communion railing.

Though we know that this is a Franciscan church, that the nuns who raised the funds for it are Franciscan, we know little about this chapel. The woman I saw postering earlier is at the back, restocking a wooden stand with candles and brochures. She's dressed in lay clothes, but something about her finally clues me in—maybe from my days long ago of taking piano lessons from the nuns, maybe the fact that she's an older woman doing this chore.

"Are you a nun?" I ask.

"Yes," she says, "I'm Sister Lauren."

And as we talk about the chapel and its history, she and Mum watch each other. They could be two old harridans, sizing each other up for religious battle; they could be a lion and a Christian. But they're not; they're two old women who have lived a lot of life.

"I'm not a Catholic," Mum says, part admission, part challenge.

"Lots aren't," says Sister Lauren.

There is sometimes this communion, I've seen it before, where old people just key into each other. They have lived that long that they know the other's story—not the specifics, but the big stories, the sheer longevity, the battles, the joys. These two women are reaching their understanding, as they laugh about lapsed Catholics and long lives and carrying on.

Then Sister Lauren asks if she can give Mum a blessing. It happens so fast and is so right that it seems she must have asked and received consent.

She leans forward, makes the sign of the cross on Mum's forehead and, while putting the other hand lightly on her hair, says something that is obviously a prayer, but the words are so unknown to me I can do nothing but catch the murmur and the blessing.

"I'll tell the sisters and we'll pray for you," she says. "You're going to be okay."

We leave the chapel, we non-religious Moirs, feeling the strength of the sisterhood at our backs.

—·—

I returned to the chapel the next day on my own. I didn't know what any of it meant—all the symbolism. Of course I understand Christ on the cross, Mary and baby Jesus, even Saint Francis of Assisi, founder of the Franciscan Order. Being there was like understanding that a rich text lay before me, but I was illiterate. It is a culture written in Italian marble, stained glass, Latin. The words of the Magnificat, the exultant prayer of Mary, were written on the chapel arch and each of the chapel's ten arched beams, symbols of sailing ships, crutches, roses: Rosa

Mystica, Mater Castissima, Consolotrix Afflictorum, Regina Angelorum, Stella Matutina, from the Litany of Loreto.

The words reminded me of my father as he long ago recited the names of the plants in Latin (*Epilobium angustifolium, Equisetum sylvaticum*). But he'd been dead seven years, and while this language brought him back to me, it was not he who occupied my heart.

The Latin words—Mater, Regina and Rosa, Consolotrix Afflictorum, consoler of the afflicted, the one who guides us through the storms of life, are maternal. Even I, with no Latin and no religion, could see and feel that.

I sat in a nun's pew, a small bench made of Appalachian oak, absorbed the silence and mystery, and wondered how much longer our Consolotrix Afflictorum would be with us.

———

In our room at the Springhill Suites across the road, I suggest to Judy that we should have a talk with Mum while we are together, before her surgery. We know about her "Do Not Resuscitate" wishes, but what if we have to make other decisions while she is unconscious?

So at the hospital, we close the door of Mum's room, and Judy opens the "come-to-Jesus" talk with Mum. We're all there: Judy, Brian, Andy, Donna and her daughter Maggie, and me. *What do you want us to do?* is what we're asking Mum. We have been in this situation before and know what decisions we may be called upon to make while she is under the anaesthetic.

What do we do if there are complications and serious risks, and they come out mid-surgery to talk to us?

Mum's sitting in her bed, looking at us, knowing we're about to have a talk.

Judy asks Mum what she wants.

"Go ahead with it," she says.

What if the odds are 40 percent that you'll die if they go ahead?

"Go ahead with it," she says.

What *about 60 percent?*

"Worth the risk," she says.

Ninety?

She looks at us, how we're trying to figure the odds and the responsibility we're about to face.

"I want them to go ahead, and if it doesn't work out, well, they'll have more information to add to their experiment."

Here we are, all us scientifically and agnostically raised kids. Dad a scientist and Mum an agnostic socialist. Earth to earth and no afterlife.

"I love you all. I've had a good life, but I can't go on like this," she says. "I don't want to die, but this is no life I'm living now."

Furthermore, she says, if she dies she doesn't want a funeral.

"You mean you don't want anything religious?" Judy asks.

"Well, that," says Mum. "But I wouldn't want you to have the expense of another trip."

"Well," Judy laughs. "If you died, we're all here anyway, so that wouldn't inconvenience anyone."

Mum grins: "Yeah, I know, but it's a lot to ask."

"We'd all need some closure," Judy says, "and so will the friends. We could do something like we did for Dad; have a gathering at the graveside and then have everyone over to the house to share stories and food."

That sounds good to Mum, who loves a good party, and then we all take turns taking pictures together and Mum looks great, far better than the rest of us.

This surgery truly is unbelievable. The young doctor explained it to us in detail the night before. He booted up the Internet on the computer in Mum's room and showed us schematic details.

But the best part is how he explained: "Yes, they do the incision in her femoral artery, and that's delicate, but get this! They use a joystick, or a steering wheel, to guide the balloon that will open the old valve, and the metal ring that will hold the valve open, and the new valve that replaces the old." He smiled as he mimicked a young kid in a bumper car, shoulders hunched and concentrating as he steers the miniature wheel. It's so complex yet so simple, and he infused us with such confidence, his skill and his youth combined with all the experience of the older cardiologist and surgeons who will work on our mother. Mum doesn't understand computers very well, but she understands people, and she was happy to see this young man's effect on all of us.

There's a team of twenty-two, from office staff to surgeons to post-operative care workers in on this. They have a lot at stake.

Early the next morning, the five of us—Judy, Brian, Andy, Donna and I—walk beside Mum's gurney to the preparation room, aiming for hope and confidence, clutching Kleenexes in our hands. Mum's the strongest one. She smiles at us; she's ready for whatever lies ahead and her smile is real.

Betty Anderson, the co-ordinator, ushers us into the family room, where other families who've travelled a long way on short notice have camped out overnight on long chesterfields.

We settle in and put on our game faces. We joke about the missing sticky cinnamon buns Betty promised us. We dig around inside the bags of snacks and silly games Cass has sent to help us through the long wait, and Brian tries out a pair of fake glasses with nose and moustache. He looks like Groucho Marx. He looks certifiable, and he gets a great laugh when he greets the surgeon, who once worked at the psychiatric hospital near Winnipeg.

The medical team reports to us regularly. The family is all here now. "It's going beautifully," they tell us. "She is amazing," they say. And we weep with relief and pride. That is our mother. Amazing. We weep with exhaustion and hope, and tears for all who have died too early in our family. And now this miracle.

They tell us her aortic valve had been almost closed, down to an opening of .23 cm. Now it is seven times larger, at 1.6 cm.

Mum is moved to the recovery room, where she will be under intensive watch for hours. We go back to the hotel to rest. After a nap and a swim in the hotel pool, I slip back to check on Mum. They let me into the recovery room but warn me she can't speak because she is intubated. That's when she begins struggling, fighting the nurses, trying to pull the horrid large tube from her throat, emerging from the anaesthetic faster than anticipated and panicking. The anaesthetist immediately approves removal of the tube. Later Judy and I visit, and Mum looks at me, takes my offered hand, and smiles.

Still drugged, she says: "I tried to tell them. I tried to tell them but they wouldn't listen!"

Judy smiles: "You won, Mom."

And then Mum says over and over before falling asleep, "I fought and I won."

———

Two days later, other heart patients who have had the traditional surgery clutch pillows against their painful sternums, as if to hold themselves together. Our little mother, like a wizened Yoda, sways easily and happily down the hospital hallway in her housecoat.

She eats like a trucker. Food she would have pushed away a few days ago, she marvels at and savours. It's like the river is reversing, or the tides, and we can see the strength flowing back into her body.

———

During the long days of recovery, while my brothers enjoy pizza at the cafeteria, I perch in the front pew at the clinic's lower-your-sodium sermon.

I solemnly take notes as they intone that too much sodium retains the fluid in your body and your heart has to work far harder to circulate everything, and trans fats narrow your arteries. There's a lot of detail, and the room is too warm, and I'm dizzy with hunger, but I see all the fun foods like bacon coagulating in my arteries like cold lard in a straw. Cast away popcorn, they say, and chips and anything fun; cast away anything worth its salt.

I am a low-sodium evangelist with a need for converts. I will inflict this new regime upon my partner, Dan. I'll pounce when he sneaks home from town with potato chips on his breath.

———

As Mum recovers and continues to astonish and charm the staff, we troop around in a clump, a slow clump, because Judy, though she's doing far better, can't walk fast in the cold air. We spend more time together than we have in years. While we know more than we want to know about the dangers of sodium and fats, almost everything in nearby restaurants is battered and deep fried and the portions of red meat are gigantic. And we crave it. Carbs and protein, salt, fat and sugar, all the sweet spots for our brains and bodies, to keep us fuelled, to keep us in good humour. Salad leaves us feeling virtuous but hungry. In the motel after a long day in the hospital, we rip into bags of pretzels and nuts, break open the wine and pop. Hash over the day and reset ourselves for the next. Andy calls Chris on the east coast of Canada; I call Dan in the west. How is the weather? How are the cats, the turtles, the dogs, the horse and donkey?

When Mum is finally ready to leave hospital, and with Judy in the driver's seat, we pile into her cherry-red van. We are like the Beverly Hillbillies. People, pillows, leftover pizza, brothers, sisters, mother, crammed in and talking over piles of stuff. We're laughing so hard, so amused with ourselves, so victorious and glorious and ridiculous that we wish everyone could have a family holiday like this.

An Agnostic Thank You

Back in St. Paul—comfortable on Dad's old green leather chair—Brian instructs Mum in the post-operative exercise routine.

"Okay, now you have to steady yourself and rise on your toes ten times," he says. "Rita, make sure she holds on," he says, happy to order me around. Here we are in our proper family positions, older ones giving the orders, younger ones the peons, getting the jobs done. It's fun, really, a family project. Every day we say, "Can you believe this?" as we see Mum grow stronger by the moment.

"I can't believe I'm breathing," she says, and we all shake our heads. The progress is phenomenal. It *is* a miracle. Sister Lauren was right: Mum is okay. Mum's better than okay; she's a phenom, a poster child. As I place my hands at her waist, I telegraph a quick agnostic thank you to a non-existent god and to the good sisters of Saint Marys for acting as messengers.

"Now Rita, tie her legs with that band," Brian instructs. Mum sits complacently, grinning, as I tie an orange rubber strap around her ankles, so she abducts one leg while the other strapped ankle creates resistance. "That's too tight," Brian bugs me from the comfort of his armchair. "Loosen it up."

"Brian, come over here and do it yourself," I say, while doing it. We could go on like this for weeks, back in the routine we knew as kids, bugging, teasing, pushing, defending each other against all outside threats, marching around our world as a team. We were always good at projects, and Mum is the perfect project.

"Okay, now, Mum, you have to do your deep breathing so you don't get pneumonia," Brian says. "Rita, get the inspirometer."

———

With all the family there to help, Judy is also able to rest and recover. Her surgery was simpler than our mother's, but involved far more post-surgical care, with sterility a major issue because the medication pumps directly into her heart. A nurse arrives daily to check for infection, and each day I see a tray of used gauze, wrappers and syringes that go into the garbage.

It's hushed at Judy's home, but we can feel the danger passing. Things have to get better. We can't manage anything more right now.

It's a huge relief that her dosage of Remodulin is on track and working. Having to wear a small pump twice the size of a large wallet, attached into her heart by a catheter tube, is awkward and annoying. She can't even remove the long tubing while in the shower. But it is doing the job; the sores on her feet are healing, all the swelling in her body is reduced, and Judy is far more grateful for the relief than downhearted about the condition it treats.

Judy gets better every day; she plays Mahjong and attends a Democratic precinct caucus meeting and her picture appears in the newspaper. I get some rest, too; Brian stays at Mum's house and the doorbell blares the "Stars and Stripes" next to his head.

We clean and sort and fix: Andy installs grab bars and other aids to help Mum in the bathroom. Brian keeps her busy with physio, helps with her daily weigh-in, washes dishes and amuses the cat. Judy's so much stronger now, that with a burst of energy she tackles Mum's basement landing, where all the canned goods are stored on narrow shelves, while I attack the basement. We agree as a baseline that anything stale-dated before the year 2000, the last century, the last millennium actually, gets tossed.

"How about this Boost from before Dad died?" she calls down the stairs to me. "It's only seven years old!" I hear it hit the garbage before I answer. "Think we could use these old margarine tubs?" Toss. "Think we need these coupons from 1997?" I know those rolls of coupons; they're stuffed in every drawer, rolled and secured with elastic bands. There are plastic bags full of plastic bags, the long plastic tubes the newspaper comes in, blue ones and orange, saved for dog walks, though the dog has been dead for years.

"What do you kids want for supper?" Mum yells from upstairs, where she's putting clothes away. She knows she can't cook for us yet, but is game for the routine. "Lobster!" Andy yells from the bathroom. "And chicken wings!" Brian yells from the living room. Judy and I know it will be leftover meatloaf and salad, but that's not the point.

Down below in Dad's old workshop, I count my progress in one-foot increments. In one week I move forward seven feet. Dad's old bandsaw blades, lethal rings of sharp rusting metal, hang from overhead water pipes. Old fluorescent lights flicker and cobwebs are strung from wall to old stone wall. I vacuum and sort. There are five glass pots from broken-down coffee makers, a wok two feet wide that Dad used for cooking huge stir-fries that were thick with pork and pineapple and cornstarch; there are aluminum pots and wire bases for Pyrex dishes that may be in a cupboard upstairs somewhere. There are cupboards and cupboards, old sheets of glass, burnt-out light tubes stacked neatly against a corner, old furniture to be fixed, old wooden boxes and tins filled with rusted screws.

I try to tune in the station on the thirty-year-old radio that's blasted loud enough for our near-deaf parents to hear for years; for when Mum came down to do laundry, or maybe the radio kept the cat company as she hunted for mice deep in the crawl spaces. I work around bags of Christmas lights and decorations, bags of unused rugs, battered old work benches with the last of Dad's tools and scraps of all varieties of wood he would use to repair some lovely old piece of furniture he found at a rummage sale.

I am overwhelmed with memories and claustrophobia.

"Ready for wine, Rit?" Judy calls down to me, and I am.

Andy and Brian return to Canada and, as Judy and Mum get better, Judy and her friends try to teach me Mahjong, which they play with laughter and cunning. We head out on another Saturday morning for an opera broadcast—Verdi's *Simon Boccanegra*—where theatregoers of a certain age flout the rules and bring in picnic baskets with wine and goodies. Sometimes it's just plain fun to be old, and know some poor young usher won't dare to kick us out for misbehaving.

At Judy's and Mum's homes, friends deliver homemade cinnamon buns and cookies and casseroles. Life is full of the aroma of rich food, hospitality and laughter, and a Super Bowl party raucous with pizza and beer.

Mum is doing well enough to be on her own. She needs to resume her independence, so I fly away and leave her to it.

——

Back home in the mountains of BC, I first notice how spacious and uncluttered our home is. I breathe deeply, glad to be back with Dan.

As the days and chores progress, I am relieved to be home but I am restless. I miss my family, the structure, the intensity of our purpose; I relive the miracle we all witnessed. I am a worshipper home from the pilgrimage and have no tolerance for the small irritants of daily life.

I write in my journal; reconfigure each day of those last weeks. Even with the best of intentions, there was never time to write while I was in Minnesota.

Dan and I buy a satellite dish so we can watch the Olympics in Vancouver, 600 km west of us: we watch Joannie Rouchette's amazing skate just after her young mother's death from a heart attack. Ice dancers Tessa Virtue and Scott Moir (Judy calls him our newfound long-lost relative) come in second in compulsories.

I need a project, so even though snow is still on the ground, every day I head outside. I haul and burn logging slash—tree limbs and debris—from all the thinning I'm doing in the forest. I need to feel useful and productive. I have to concentrate and be careful while using the chainsaw; it's demanding. There is moss and rock and slash to trip on, but I'm using my body how I want to, am completely focussed and see the tangible results of my labour. I see where all the small fir wants to release its youth and energy amidst the spindly, strangling and dying pine, see where the elk have been from their droppings, so much bigger than that of the deer.

An old neighbour down the road burns grass along his fenceline, so I stop to talk and he asks about Mum, then catches me up on various animal news. A cougar has been killed that had been preying on neighbourhood sheep. He's seen day-old cougar tracks on the field of our community hall. One day all the wild turkeys and local deer ran across that field, and he went to check and saw three bobcats after them, a rare sighting even in our rural valley. With every story, I feel more at home, settling in to who we are, so different from my urban family's daily life.

I try my best to reimmerse myself in a long-overdue writing project, a photo history book of the Slocan Valley, which my publisher has been more than patient about while I've been with my family. But still, even with deadlines to firm me up, I cannot find my feet, in my home life or in work. After all, I have been to Lourdes, and paying the Telus bill, getting the oil changed, and grinding away at photo captions doesn't pass muster.

Several nights I dream I am back at my mother's house, wake up thinking I'm with her, but it is only Dan's restlessness and his own worries that trigger my alarm system, still on hyper alert after so long. We are in the dregs of winter, and spring cannot come soon enough.

But winter hangs on and on. I have trouble writing, with doing just about anything except using my chainsaw.

I miss Judy. I miss us together in the aftermath of crisis. We have come through this one, and Mum is doing fine, but I think of how Judy and I weathered so much; four deaths in six years: her husband, Mike, in 1997, her stepson John in 2001, her son William in 2002, our father in 2003. And now this close call with Mum. Each time, I made the trek to Minnesota to stay with her and we rebuilt and moved on with our lives.

And through this, no matter the immediacy of the crises we faced over the decades, Judy supported my ongoing work as a writer. She listened to me as I crawled my way through each manuscript and then she hosted book launches for each one.

She invited her many friends and catered the food. My mother and sister Donna, both experienced in retail, set up the sales table. And I got to be the star.

In the big room where the weddings took place, I read the stories of travels with my mother across the prairies and en route to Nova Scotia. As the years went on, I wrote more stories of our family, our politics, our celebrations and catastrophes. In Judy's home, in front of family and friends, I read the story of the plane crash that killed her son William along with the senator everyone in the room knew and loved. I read them stories of our mother's birth and our father's death.

Judy made sure they knew me as the writer from Canada, that the epithet "Judy's sister" wasn't always the first descriptor. She was proud of me. She encouraged and applauded me. She listened and helped me through the decisions I was edging toward. They were my own decisions, but she could see into me deeply, could probe the hard spots, release the doubts and pain and bank them with laughter.

This is the sisterhood I miss when we are apart. The powerful sisterhood of Judy.

Judy and I were both part of that greater sisterhood, too. Both feminists, both community organizers and activists. She supported women's rights and gay rights and many other causes and ran for political office. On her sixtieth birthday she was awarded the key to her city.

She spearheaded the historic preservation and revival of

her derelict neighbourhood, heading a community organization that rebuilt with parks and group homes, restored historic buildings, and worked for affordable housing and a strong retail sector. All this in a neighbourhood once so crime-riddled that the police warned her and her husband that they shouldn't move there if they had children.

She has a temper, I know that. A taut and sharp anger honed from years of activism and earning her stripes. She could take a politician from her own party to task, because she knew politics and the party inside out, top to bottom. She'd done all the jobs, from door knocking and brochure folding to working as a senior staffer in the Legislature, to throwing huge fundraisers and running for office. People returned her calls, and if they didn't, they'd be wiping their own shit off their shoes. And for that same person, eventually, if they got their act back together, got their politics back on the right and courageous path, she'd throw another fundraiser and help them on their way.

—

Some time after William's death in the plane crash in 2002 that killed the senator and all on board, I stayed with Judy long enough to help with a few weddings. As I mopped the main room where the buffets were set out, Judy pushed through the swinging door from the kitchen, in her hand the printed program for that weekend's reception.

"You won't believe this," she said. She passed me the program, pointed to the *in memoriam* passage, where I recognized the name of one of the pilots found responsible for the crash. The horrific crash was a huge story in the life of Minnesotans, the investigation with the names of the pilots and the passengers in the news every day for months afterward, and Judy, as mother of one of the victims, was interviewed often.

Now, in her home, she would be hosting the wedding for this pilot's family.

We stared at the name.

"They haven't made the connection," she said.

"Oh, Jude," I said, "This is unreal."

"Yeah."

I looked at the rest of the program and passed it back to her.

"What are you going to do?"

"Nothing," she said. "This is between you and me."

We didn't tell anyone. We worked as hard as or harder than ever to make that wedding perfect. It was that family's special day and Judy was determined that nothing should take away from it. There was never a moment's hesitation about how we would proceed. I don't know what it cost her emotionally to do that, or if it gave her strength to know she could.

——

If she has weaknesses, I don't see them. She's my big sister and she symbolizes strength and fairness. She balances the hard grinding detail work of a campaign or catering a wedding with wine and laughter, or the quiet hours reading a book on the deck at the lake.

I realize my own style of organizing is similar to hers. Consultation and crisis prevention supplemented with food and drink and laughter. Though I hate conflict, and avoid it by meticulous preparation and negotiation, there are times my anger surfaces. Sometimes as a rant, sometimes as a cold and fierce denunciation of the offender. And though I wish I could do it more, I can sometimes say honestly: "Well, that's tomorrow's problem," and go on to enjoy the rest of my day.

⎯

In St. Paul, a month after her surgery, Mum strides forty laps around her house. Judy drives her to cardio-physio three times a week. "I wonder if I should get a personal trainer at the Y?" Mum muses to me over the phone, and her determination and my laughter and delight at her recovery are the inspiration I need to slough off my own winter ennui.

I clean my office, dust ledges, vacuum cat hair, sort and toss old paper. I need a fresh slate.

Then I call Sister Lauren. It seems so alien, almost sacrilegious, to dial up a nun from something as mundane as a telephone. As if I should only attempt contact through prayer, or by smoke signal. To my astonishment, they page Sister Lauren from the halls of Saint Marys. I imagine her striding down the passages, her black habit flowing, though I don't recall that she ever wore such traditional garb.

"Sister Lauren?" I ask. "I don't know if you remember us..." I begin tentatively.

When I tell her the details, she does remember; the thank-you card Mum and I sent is on the desk in front of her. She asks how Mum is doing, and if there's something I need help with.

"Do you remember what prayer you said for my mother?"

"It was the blessing of St. Francis," she says.

"Could you say it for me so I can write it down?"

And she does, slowly in her old and kind voice:

May the Lord bless you and keep you

May he turn his face toward you

And grant you his peace.

Once again I feel her calm, even her authority, strengthening my bones.

—

Moir and Virtue win gold. Our women's and men's hockey teams both win gold. Dan and I yip and holler at the TV set, so happy for our people. I email back and forth with my small coterie of fanatical figure-skating friends, rave about amazing lifts, a triple Lutz or a throw triple Salchow. Joannie Rouchette skates for bronze, and we join the nation in support, as if she can hear us weeping and cheering for her.

I place recipe books in the cupboard Dan built while I was away. Two years ago, after living back and forth in each of our houses for six years, Dan and I decided to live together. He moved into my neighbourhood and built a house and, when we were ready, we added on a dining room and a large office for me. I work many odd jobs, editing, being a secretary, cleaning houses, whatever comes along to pay the bills, but want all the time possible at home. Each day I take long walks; I sign up for a yoga course with special emphasis on opening up the heart.

Out in the forest, I fire up the Husq'varna chainsaw Dan gave me for Christmas. I know many people would find that an odd gift to give a woman, but I love chainsaws. I love Husq'varnas, the bright orange, the solid strong body that does such good work. I love the decompression button that makes starting it such a pleasure. And then, in my workboots and work clothes, I thin hundreds of small pine, spindly tall sick trees that grew like crowded weeds after this area was clear-cut decades ago. Amidst them, small fir struggle for light, and I release them to air and water. I love the small pines, keep many of them, because no other trees move as they do in the wind. They are lithe; they sway like dancers in a line, can bend close to the ground and swing back up. But there are too many and they are dying.

I call on friends to help haul the slash to a bonfire, and Dan and I get out the smokies and cold beer; we drag treetops to our firepit and buck the larger sections into rounds of firewood to warm our home later in the year.

———

We all restore our lives. In Nova Scotia, Andy plays boogie-woogie at Freeport's restaurant, Lavena's Catch, and I love to imagine him there with Chris, eating haddock and chips, Andy at the piano, Chris visiting friends and taking pictures for the village paper, *Passages*. In Winnipeg, Brian returns to his demanding job as a probation officer. Judy improves at Mahjong, laughing and carrying on. Donna, her husband, Steve, and their daughters Erin and Maggie plant their backyard garden. Mum walks around the block and astounds the neighbours.

—

Despite the carpentry work to build this new home, and my work in the forest, I am not settled. It feels like a stage waiting for the script to be written. It is so unlike my mother's and sister's homes, where the boards are well-trodden, the actors know their lines, and the play is in full gear.

When Dan and I moved from our long-time homes in our old forests to this very different site, it was an exciting but difficult upheaval. He had lived on a steep mountainside with a waterfall and creek, huge cedars and dark cool places. I lived for thirty-four years next to my community centre, the Vallican Whole, serving as its caretaker and groundskeeper, in a log house I built with my partner of the time. The forest was dark and lush with spring runoff creeks and magnificent with mature cedar and fir, yew with its red berries, birch and quaking aspen, hemlock with its delicate green leader, larch and giant spruce. The scent of wild ginger permeated the cool forest, and Indian pipe grew along the damp paths, its ghostly stems speaking of the dead leaves, rich with nutrients, mulching below me as I walked barefoot. Judy and her family visited me in my old log house; my father and mother, then Brian, and then my mother and sisters together. My log house was filled with memories; this new home Dan and I built is still barren. My family has never visited.

It sits on a flat site, once logged over and full of the spindly pine and some weary cedar that can't take the sun. True, there are stately fire-resistant ponderosa pine on the hillside, their long clusters of needles sweeping and regal. There are a few fir large enough to provide shade in the heat of the day.

We are bereft of the mystery of our dark forests; but we realize how little light we had in our old homes and we build a house made of windows, so many windows that there is hardly room to hang a painting.

The year before my mother's surgery, we had been laying floors, ripping, routering, sanding and painting trim for the fifty windows. My office alone has eleven windows and two skylights. I feel like I'm back on the prairies, flooded with light.

Our move into this house was so recent that cookbooks still wait in boxes, the whole process abandoned as I left for Minnesota.

And outside is still a mess: thousands of rocks from this land, which was an old riverbed, have been disturbed and strewn by construction. The land is rough and dry, destroyed as a forest decades ago without the transition to anything else. Unlike our old forests, this land is more an anecdote than a novel, and I don't know where to start. I crave structure and security, but instead struggle to find my pace, to settle down when everything's unsettled. I phone Judy and talk about the forest, about the book I am working on, the right menu for a big event coming up where I am head cook; they're all my way of belonging, of burrowing into my place.

Judy doesn't know much about forests, except the woods at the family lake place and what she absorbed from our botanist father; but she knows that serving and opening your doors to people creates a home, or a haven for community, for laughter, discussion and action. And with thirty or more years as a caterer, she's a smart, efficient planner. Her voice, her assurance, our stories as we plan, are what I need and what I can count on.

"Jude?"

"Yeah?" she says.

I hear her thousands of kilometres away as she cradles the phone to her ear, slams the fridge door in her big kitchen and rams a screwdriver in to hold the latch closed properly.

"I want to hold a St. Patrick's Day breakfast for a fundraiser, but I need to pick your brain."

"Sure, what's on the menu? Blood pudding?"

She's referring to our trip to Ireland a decade ago, with Donna and Mum. The four of us together for the first time in years, on a trip to Mother's spiritual, ancestral and mythical homeland.

We tried to eat white pudding and black pudding, coagulated cooked blood from a pig, for Mum's sake, to show her we were really trying. Once.

"How many people are you expecting?"

I hear her settle down, scraping a wooden chair out from the big round wooden table.

"Sixty to a hundred."

"Just a second," she says, "I need a pen." And she's off to her office to grab a note pad and felt tip.

For Judy, serving sixty to a hundred is no effort. But for me, these larger groups take some thinking. You want it attractive but easy, the hot food hot and the cold food cold, and for the serving to be practical.

"Are you doing hot food?"

"Yeah, we have two ovens, and warming pans and stuff."

"What about potatoes?"

In Ireland we had potatoes with everything; once at a pub our chips arrived with a side order of boiled potatoes.

"You could do potatoes-in-the-oven. I make that all the time for the mayor's breakfast here on St. Patrick's Day. You've had it here, right?"

Yes, I've had it at Judy's, for the mayor's breakfast, or during the St. Paul marathon, when the neighbourhood congregated at her house for breakfast, and sometimes strangers walked in as well, to heap their plates with potatoes and eggs before the marathoners ran by at the end of their route.

In Ireland at night, we ate in pubs. Each day or two we drove to a new village, always on narrow roads. Unexpectedly, I was the only qualified driver. Judy couldn't drive a standard,

Donna couldn't drive at all, and the rental company disqualified Mum due to her age, seventy-eight at the time. Judy was my navigator, and at first it was all nerve-wracking. Driving on the left taxed all my normal responses, and the roads were so narrow and winding that I didn't leave second gear for the first week. But then we'd reach our destination and find a B&B listed in a guidebook. We had no cell phones back then. While Donna and Mum napped, Judy and I, the advance party, mapped out pubs, music, theatre and food for the evening. It was two hours of absolute laughter, two women who travelled at the same speed, discovering a different small world together every afternoon and planning the evening.

"Okay, potatoes. What else?" I ask.

Mum wanted to go everywhere and, at some point, we had to have a talk. We couldn't retrace all the steps she'd taken in her three previous trips to Ireland. And besides, revisiting would never be the same as discovering something together.

We decided that each of us would choose one place or one event that absolutely mattered. Mum wanted Castlebar in County Mayo, so we could meet our fourth cousin, Ann Kelly. Donna chose the Blarney Stone. I wanted the Giant's Chair above the ocean where I could throw my dog Connor's ashes. To fulfill her husband's wish before he died, Judy chose the pilgrimage to an old friend's tumbled-down stone house where the sheep sheltered by the ocean.

"What about soda bread?"

Mum learned to make soda bread. In her Irish cottage in St. Paul, with Irish music playing, as she baked she would say: I would like to die in Ireland, or I would like to move there, and we all thought, Where? How? As if she could never be satisfied with where she was, as if Winnipeg, or St. Paul, wasn't truly home. That a place she'd never been for more than three weeks, where her ancestors had left decades ago, was really home. Perhaps the pull of our ancestors' homeland was stronger than I could understand.

"Yeah, you could do soda bread. And scones."

Judy says *scones* as if it rhymes with stones. I say *scones* with a soft "o." But I don't correct her.

"What else, do you think?"

"Guinness? Remember Donna and the Guinness sign?"

In Dublin, we stopped outside one of the many pubs that served Guinness; they all served Guinness; decided to go our own ways for a few hours, to take a break from the constant togetherness and meet two hours later at the same spot. Back then Judy could walk fast and look at the architecture; Mum, with her retail experience, was keen on window displays, and I could look at public sculpture and art. Donna said she'd be fine and see us later. She and Mum later found each other, met up with a nice man who escorted them through streets and alleys.

Donna said she knew where we were meeting; she just had to find the Guinness sign. Maybe she didn't realize how many there were, but the two of them were charmed. Shamrocks drifted from their shoulders; the music of harps guided their way.

"Scones and Irish coffee. And music," I add.

"Sounds good," Judy says, and we both think about a street festival that really wasn't for tourists, and got loud and rowdy as dark descended. How we knew we didn't belong there and slipped away, safe with each other as drunks began shouting and throwing beer bottles and the music grew crazed.

"Wish I could be there," she says. "Let me know how it goes."

"Sláinte, Jude. Love you."

"Love you, too."

———

Aside from my contact with Judy and my cooking for the community event, I remain off-kilter. So while Dan is away visiting his family, my long-time friend Lynne Van Luven comes to stay. She is a fiendish gardener, writer, teacher and an old prairie woman like me.

Many of my best women friends, I begin to understand, are just slightly older than me. As if unwittingly I seek a familiar pattern.

"I love the light," Lynne says. She walks the two acres with me and, while I feel confined after the twelve acres I lived on before, and daunted by the piles of stones and the thick layers of dry duff and needles, by the dead and broken branches everywhere, she sees only possibilities.

My imagination is limited to the depth of the hole we can dig to bury all these bloody round rocks. They're not beautiful with vivid colours and jagged crystal; they are boring round river rocks.

"Think of them as a resource instead of a nuisance," she says. "You don't have a river? Let's build a dry riverbed. Let's build rock gardens."

We rake piles of slash, build bonfires and drink wine and talk all night. She builds an entire rock garden while I'm at work one day, and we lay out rock rivers in the natural contours of the land. Old mounds of excavated dirt we shape into coulees, as if we're both back in southern Alberta where we first met. When she leaves, instead of being hooded with disappointment, my eyes have been opened.

Lynne is right. There is so much more sun here. And the wind soughing through the pines. When I was a young woman I longed for everything old, an old-fashioned log cabin, a home in the deep woods with huge mature forest. I soaked in its longevity, its wisdom; but now I am older myself and relish young. After Lynne's visit, I walk around this property many times; my cat follows so she too can explore the change in her universe. I see the eager young fir soaking in the light in the large openings; the pine fingers like Christmas tree candles shooting straight up before they settle down to become mature branches. My old land didn't need me anymore. I didn't have the stamina to put anything new into it, to fix my old house, to keep constant watch on the community hall and its needs. This land is private, needs work, and challenges me. Each time I place a rock just so, or rake down to new earth, it's like I'm giving the land a good back scratch that makes everything better.

———

My mother is back in gear, full of her usual piss and vinegar. On the phone I tell her I went to a dance alone at the Vallican Whole when Dan was away. Lots of women danced together and it was fun.

"Things have progressed so much," she philosophizes. "When I was young, you had to dance with a male. It was so boring sometimes and it gave them an overinflated sense of themselves."

———

My mother is launched and I realize it is me who needs help right now, with the land, with my photo history book, with my emotions. Somehow after all the time in Minnesota and with my family, the structure of the hospital and the routines, and even given the recent work with Lynne, I can't find my own drive. At my request, my publisher brings in an editor who comes to my new home office and kindly and firmly kicks me in the ass. Why did I care about this history book? she asks, other than guilt about not getting it done and disappointing the people who shared their precious photographs? She pushes me with questions: What is your passion? What is the book's drive? She gives me a day to figure it out, then returns and pushes me harder, and I force myself to focus; I think about structure, how in the cities, there is long-established structure and institutions, but in the rural areas, we have to invent it all. I think about how and why we do that, how we succeed and sometimes fail.

I dig out my passion for my community and write a statement about what makes us tick, where we all come from and how we fight and compromise, how we hate each other sometimes, but love and support each other through deaths and births, how we help each other's children grow up, or help bury them if they die before us, how we survive through the big waves and movements, wars and immigration, through all our petty differences and struggles. The editor is happy and I'm ready to roll.

On the spur of the moment, on a day's notice, I throw a thirty-fifth anniversary party for myself. Thirty-five years to the day since I moved to this valley and built the log caretaker's house that itself has now become an institution along with the Vallican Whole it serves. The history book I'm working on nudges me to consider my own part in history. How I once was young but now am becoming part of the history, becoming one of the historians.

Over the summer I work madly and happily to meet my deadline, excited and inspired. At the same time, Dan and I stain all the larch siding and then, as the first coat of grey stucco is applied, we take off for St. Paul. Dan is with me and I am so glad. He loves my family and I want to hear his laughter mingle with theirs. I love the sound of Judy and Dan laughing together.

A few years ago, the three of us took a road trip to the southeastern US. We had abandoned any attempt to travel lightly. As we watched others check into hotels with one small kit bag, we'd roll our laden cart to the elevator. Suitcases and walking shoes, pillows, bathing suits and books and pajamas. Maybe a radio. A cooler with cheese and fruit and chicken. The bottles of wine and glasses. Coats for cool nights. Toiletries. Cameras. Guidebooks and histories.

The hotels were so predictable with their rolling luggage carts, complete with brass rod for hanging suits. The Samuel Clemens Inn in Hannibal, Missouri, the Holiday Inn Express in Nashville, Tennessee. All fine places, but hardly worth retelling. It's the story of the Winner's Circle in Georgetown, Kentucky, that Judy told and retold, her laughter so infectious it drew those on the periphery in to listen.

We'd spent a full day in Lexington, searching out Dan's long-lost relatives in a big cemetery, as we'd searched years earlier for his long-lost relatives in Nova Scotia. It's fun to have a grail, but at the end of a hot afternoon, we headed for Georgetown, Judy driving, Dan in front with her, and me in the back amidst guidebooks and coupons, avid for deals. I muttered away, turning pages and reading aloud, so Dan and Judy could speculate upon what appalling place I—always on the lookout for ma and pa motels rather than corporate chains—would discover.

"The Winner's Circle," I proclaimed, slapping the page. "Regular $39. With this coupon, $32."

Groans from the front seat, all the encouragement I needed.

"Family operated!"

Groan.

"Character!"

"God spare us."

"Charm! Pictures of Kentucky Derby horses in the corridors!"

"Should we let her have her way?" Judy asks Dan.

"She'll just whinge if we don't."

The Winner's Circle was... unprepossessing. But, coupon in hand, I jumped out of the van and ran in like the good advance party I am, to wheel out the luggage cart. Judy and Dan opened the van's back door and prepared to unload.

"They don't have a luggage cart!" I raced out to report. "They'll find something else!"

The ancient mariner at the desk lifted himself slowly from the chair, hands braced on the edge of the check-in counter.

"You can go look in there," his finger of doom pointing to a closed room. "Maybe something in there," he yelled slowly. Perhaps my clipped Canadian accent and my strange request for a luggage cart prompted his hand gestures and exaggerated slowness.

From the midden of old lamps, broken bed frames and discarded coffee makers, I wrested my squeaking and bent treasure, then exited backward into the parking lot, hiding my face, smiling so hard it hurt.

The grocery cart I wheeled was bent and off balance and screeching. I looked up to Judy and Dan over the racket and their united groan, their rolling eyes told me I'd accomplished the very best; Judy laughing so hard I thought I would never be happier. We loaded that mangled cart with all our stuff, pushed it rakishly down the hallway of outdated photos, and the next morning couldn't get the showers to work. It was the worst deal I'd ever found. But the best.

On our journey we'd been to the source of Mark Twain's stories. We'd witnessed the Atlantic Ocean in its full force. We toured historic mansions, saw fine plays with local casts, enjoyed wonderful food. But it's the laughter at my hunt for the good deal, the grocery cart in the parking lot at the Winner's Circle that tops the story list every time. People asked Judy to repeat it. They knew the beginning and they knew the end. But they wanted it again. It was so full of love and teasing; an explosion of sweetness and tears. It is the essence of who we were together; sophistication and innocence dancing our way into heaven.

——

In Minnesota, Dan, Mum and I spend a glorious afternoon at the family cabin, wading, swimming and birdwatching. We see a bald eagle, pelicans and gulls, a ring-necked pheasant, a red-bellied sapsucker, wild turkeys and all the usual resident chickadees and grosbeaks, warblers and goldfinches. Mum explores the sandy shore, harvesting shells.

We treat my niece Maggie to the musical *Oliver!* at the Como Park Pavilion. We board an old paddlewheeler for a tour of the Mississippi River. As we walk across the park to board the vessel, it's surprising that Judy can't keep up with Mum. "I forgot my cane," Mum calls back to us. "I have to go fast or I'll lose my balance!" It would be a celebration of Mum's recovery if we weren't so obviously witnessing Judy's increasing struggle.

⸺

A few days later, knowing Judy didn't want a birthday party, doesn't need "things" and that she's catering an event for a friend that day, Dan, Mum and I secretly bake cookies, decorate them and jumble them up in a tin. Each cookie is coated in coloured icing with one letter or number. Like giggling teenagers, we invite Judy over and she sorts the cookies on Mum's table: it takes just long enough for us to be delighted that our subterfuge has succeeded. The cookies spell out our wish: HAPPY 65th JUDY, JULY 18, 1945. Her surprise and happiness with this simple gift is all we could ever want. It's the picture of Judy's laughter and delight, the cookies spread out before her, that I want to look at every time I miss her.

⸺

Judy's doctor wanted her back in hospital to drain the fluid from her legs and from around her heart and lungs. No, she tells her doctor, not until Rita and I have done something special together.

We'd done lots of fun things with my mother and Dan and my nieces and nephew, but Judy and I hadn't done anything special on our own. While her friends treated Dan to a Minnesota Twins game, Judy and I headed to the history centre just a few blocks from her home.

I didn't even know that we were both Beatles fans; that's how little time we'd spent together as teenagers. When the Beatles stormed North America in the 1960s, I was a teeny-bopper and she was older, sophisticated and living on campus during her first year of university. I was twelve years old screaming my head off with hundreds of other girls in the lineup for *A Hard Day's Night* at the Fargo movie theatre, while she entered leadership training in ROTC, the Reserve Officer Training Corps.

I didn't know that the Beatles had played in Minneapolis in 1965; and now, forty-five years later, the Minnesota History Center was celebrating with a photo exhibit, book launch and tribute band.

Judy could barely walk for the swelling in her ankles and feet, but she insisted she could do it. We parked as close as possible and I carried the canvas folding chairs. She had to rest often, but took the stairs a few at a time up to the outdoor plaza. She never complained for a moment. Like me, she was excited, in a crowd of revved-up Beatlemaniacs who could hardly wait for the music.

The band started, and we sang every word: "She Loves You" and "I Wanna Hold Your Hand" and "Yesterday." The songs of our lives, the songs we could sing with each other, to each other. We knew things weren't right in her body. She knew it more than I ever did. But in that moment, everything was right. We danced together, ever so briefly, or at least that's what I want to remember. We ate hot dogs and chips and we sang and laughed, our own little island, two sisters.

I helped my sister down the stairs, ferrying souvenirs and chairs to the car, taking her arm.

"Hey Jude," they sang. Hey Jude. Don't be afraid.

———

She was back in hospital; Dan and I offered to change our flights to stay longer, but she said, no, there's lots of people here with me. You've been here and it's been great, but go home and live your lives. I'll be fine.

Judy stayed in University Hospital far longer than expected. On the phone her voice was tired, that voice from deep inside that understood this time there wasn't a new solution to be found. Her disease was called CREST syndrome, a kind of systemic sclerosis. It stands for Calcinosis, Raynaud's phenomenon, Esophageal dysmotility, Sclerodactyly and Telangiectasia, though of course it's a jumble of words and much of this I came to understand later. The first symptoms were cold hands and feet, Raynaud's, poor circulation. Eventually the disease progressed to her heart and lungs. One year her heart was good, and the next year it wasn't. She was diagnosed with pulmonary hypertension. There was the surgery, attaching the catheter and Remodulin pump. Somehow the disease had entered her intestines, and during one crisis she almost bled to death; she was

down to 4.5 litres of blood when the normal amount for her size
would have been 11. That time the ambulance had to come to
the back door of her home; she made the request for no siren,
because on the main floor her son David was catering a huge
wedding; the family rule ruled: a wedding party should never
learn of a crisis in the midst of their celebration.

In the last year, she'd been hospitalized for a total of three
months. They performed a thoracotomy; created a "window"
which allowed fluids to drain directly into her body instead of
building up in her heart. It was a serious surgery, and thousands
of kilometres away from her, I slid into deep fear and grieving,
fell apart pretty much, afraid for my Judy; our Judy. I was so glad
Dan had just been to St. Paul with me, because while he is gen-
erally a stolid "wait and see" kind of guy, he had seen the decline
in her health and understood the cause of my fear.

When Judy was home, she gained strength quickly. She
planted her garden, sat in the sun and read, went out with
friends. We lived so far apart, were so close but so separate. I
could not bear what lay ahead. But, of course, I had to bear what
lay ahead.

I had to most fervently work at not believing in God. I
would have split atoms; I would split infinitives, not to believe.
It would have been so easy to slide there, dog paddle in those
soothing, drifting waters. To pray to a higher power.

And so I moved rocks. Where I wanted waters to swirl
in my pretend rivers, I chose rocks with swirl in them. Some

sections shift rapidly from smooth to broken, from soothing grey-blue rocks near spikey blue fescues to jagged red rocks near the Japanese blood grass. In other places, I mounded gentle hillsides, my small coulees cascading with wild blue lupins, drifts of columbine, the poppy opiate of orange.

One time it seemed she had a cold and flu, but really she was bleeding to death inside.

Japanese blood grass.

Another time no drugs or intravenous miracles would remove the water from around her heart, and there was another surgery. Another time there's something close to dialysis.

Swollen rivers.

She'll have been doing fine, living her life, and then something goes wrong and she's packed her bag for the hospital.

I search out large rocks. I plant blowing grasses and plumes of Russian sage.

And I work most fervently at not begging to God.

———

To pay the bills, I work the usual part-time jobs: secretarial, cleaning the Vallican Whole after events, doing publicity for touring authors. I stain more siding boards for the house, and make the first major deadline for my history book, *The Third Crop*. The title symbolizes endurance: the hard work, skill and luck that mean you can harvest a third crop off your fields to help feed your livestock through the winter. I interview many people, sit at their kitchen tables, where they serve me egg salad sandwiches and tell me their stories and those of their ancestors and neighbours. I am documenting their lives, and they have entrusted me.

All through this process, I feel I am on hold, my heart and mind really on Judy's health, but I have to keep moving. I'm documenting history, something you'd think is solid, static, a concrete foundation. But when you write a local history, it is so easy to get small details wrong, and everyone will make sure you hear about it. They'll stop you at the Co-op as you buy milk. They'll call you at home. As my family story matters to me, I want to get their family stories right, too. Because history is not static; it is alive, the undercurrent as we bob on the surface. So I dive in, swim deep, find the slipstream of stories through sheer hard and demanding work. I check facts repeatedly, review every photo and every caption with every family, with archives and museums, cross-check with newspaper articles and previous books written about the Doukhobors and the miners; native history and labour history; farmers and trappers and school teachers. I can't just chunk them around as if they're cardboard cutouts. I have to concentrate hard enough so the people I'm looking at in the photos begin to help me, as if they can feel my intelligence speaking to theirs, as if they know I am listening to them and that if I truly believe they matter, that their stories aren't just a way to pass my time, they will help me discover the path of the story. The work is exacting but exciting as I immerse myself in my own community's lives and struggles; find the storyline and sense of movement, as the faces and stories come to life. I know I have to do this, as much as I would wish to go live by my sister's side. Writing is my lifeline, my tow rope, my sail.

——

Dan and I choose semolina, the lovely colour of yellow wheat, for our final coat of stucco. We're absolutely hopeless about colour after decades in our brown houses in the dark woods, but have to make these choices; it's discombobulating, confusing and fun. We set foot-square samples of coloured stucco along an outside wall, and check them every few hours to see how they respond to the changing light and cloud cover. It becomes obvious which has a tinge of orange and will hold its warmth. Another sample may look stunning in one light, but become muddy as the light shifts. We choose the semolina because it makes me smile every time I look at it. Then I locate three young larch trees growing along a nearby road and transplant them near the house. They'll turn golden yellow every autumn, and they, too, will pass the happiness test.

——

After my manuscript goes off to the editor, I return to St. Paul, the third trip this year, for another big transition. Judy and I have to help Mum move into assisted living. Although Mum's health is good, she experiences more and more difficulty living alone, and Judy is in and out of hospital too often to be counted upon to support Mum's needs. My sister Donna doesn't drive, her husband is sick, and it's all too much. But Mum knows it's time to make the change and requires our help to do it. There are too many decisions to be made; too much stuff to get rid of, despite all our earlier efforts.

She can't keep up with the cleaning, won't let the cleaning lady do the bedroom or the bathroom. Her porch is unnavigable with outside plants she's brought inside. Hibiscus battles for space with overwintering geraniums and a six-foot Norfolk pine in a huge heavy pot; small tables and ledges are crammed with teddy bears, knick-knacks and oxalis, all tangled with hanging succulents and spider plants. Bookshelves are wedged solid with volumes on Ireland and the Kennedys.

Every day she tries to sort and get rid of clutter, but she can't manage. It's overwhelming. It exhausts her and she becomes anxious and tense. She stuffs plastic bags with stuff and shoves the bags into already overcrowded cupboards.

She gets confused about keys. She opens her front door to strangers because they look honest. She worries about Judy and doesn't want to be a burden.

When Judy is not hospitalized, she comes with us to three of the five assisted living facilities we visit. We assure Mum there is no urgency, but there is.

As our lives narrow to making appointments and finding our way to seniors' residences, or at Mum's house discarding old margarine containers, the bigger world out there somewhere goes on. In the US mid-term elections, the Democrats get wiped out, with the Republicans taking the House of Representatives, hundreds of state elections, and most of the governors' races. The right-wing Tea Party gains more and more power, and fear and screaming television and radio hosts are king. Canada seems farther and farther away. What I hear of Canada is only the weather: a cold front is sweeping down from Canada. That is Canada, the big cold front.

I can't keep up with life back home, exchange only short late-night emails with Dan, don't even check the websites of Canadian papers or the CBC. I don't have any spare energy to know anything more than the domestic front in my mother's and sister's homes.

―――

When we go to check out the old folks' homes, Mum dresses up; she wears a knitted tam, an Irish tweed cape or a bulky knit sweater with wooden buttons from County Mayo, and flannel pants. She walks briskly, using the cane Dad made for her, her name hand-etched around the top in a small band of copper.

Before we leave her tiny front porch, I hold her cane while she locks the door. She passes me the keys as I pass her the cane. Judy's well-heated van is close to Mum's front steps; Mum gets in the passenger side, places her cane beside her and her purse securely on her lap. I return her house keys, which she puts into the specific spot in her purse. This meticulous key and cane ritual completed, I grapple with the seat belt for her to fasten, then we're off.

The places we visit are all very nice. They are clean and the staff is good and the people seem contented. Dining rooms are spacious and comfortable. But there is always something just not right. Mum can't take her cat unless it is declawed; in others she can't take her cat at all. She says they are all "lovely," but we know her tone of voice. She wants to be helpful, she knows this move is necessary, she knows how awful it is for families when their parents refuse to move, and she wants time while she's still healthy to adjust to a big change. But the niceness of the places is the problem. It's not nice she wants; it's character. These places are clean and well appointed, ye olde oak and ruffle: Corporate Colonial.

And then, on a day when Judy's in the hospital and can't be with us, Mum and I walk into The Wellington.

At first you wonder, *hmm*, back a block behind the McDonald's just off a major thoroughfare. But you get back just that one block and you're in an old neighbourhood with huge trees, a kids' playground with swings and climbing bars, old houses and new ones, just a few blocks from the Mississippi River.

"Are you going to come live with us?" asks a husky-voiced woman sitting outside in her wheelchair. "We're fun. You'll like it here."

I wonder if she is paid to sit out there, a kind of advertisement. But no, she's real; it's all real, as I begin to understand as Mum and I make our way through.

The Wellington is a nine-storey apartment building

converted into assisted living. Residents sit in the main area, not to wait for a relative to pick them up or for the bus trip to the mall: they're hanging out visiting each other, drinking coffee, reading the paper.

On the eighth floor, a corner suite has recently been vacated. Smoking used to be allowed, the manager Craig explains unnecessarily as the walls exude the unmistakable acrid smell. They will replace the carpet throughout, repaint the rooms, re-tile the bathroom. In spite of the lingering odour, something clicks for Mum. Light floods the suite; large opening windows with big ledges look out over the river valley.

The cat would like those, she says.

Maybe the couch could go there, she says, pointing to a long wall. She walks ahead of me into the bedroom. The bed could go here, she says, and looks at me in a way that tells me this is it. As she looks out over the Mississippi River, at the maples and oak in their full colour, in this room flooded with prairie light, she is certain.

Downstairs on the main floor there's a baby grand piano, a huge fish tank, a big dining room and an exercise room. You can feel the life here, people doing things in every room—tai chi, a history lecture, people playing cards, doing social things Mum doesn't do now but might. And there is room to walk inside or out; decks with summertime chairs, lots of plants, and some people have small dogs. It feels like a community.

She is done with being trapped in a house she loves but

can barely step outside of for the Minnesota winter and the ice. She wants to walk miles a day, inside the building or out, to go to her exercise classes again, to find people to visit and laugh with.

We report to Judy that this may be the place.

Hey Jude: 2011

The moving van gets stuck in the lane behind Mum's old house. They have a hell of a time manoeuvring furniture past her chair lift, which narrows the stairs. David wheels favourite old lamps and plants in a grocery cart into The Wellington's elevator and through the hallways to Mum's suite, then wheels them out again when inevitably they overwhelm the space. After Mum is settled and ready for a nap in her new bedroom, we return to the carriage house; wearing heavy gloves and uttering bad words, we shove the brawling cat head-first into a carrier and later tell Mum it went smoothly.

Then we all drink wine.

———

Dan and I take our first winter holiday to a warm place. Everywhere in Canada is cold, so he suggests Nevada or somewhere quiet and desert-like. I crave music, street life, culture and great food. We head for New Orleans.

We ask Judy if she wants to join us because she loves the city, and we have such fun travelling together, but she says, "No, it's a city for walking, and I can't do that right now. You two go and you'll love it."

We deliberately arrive the day after Mardi Gras. It takes a day for the littered streets to be cleaned up, for musicians to recover from hangovers, but soon the early St. Patrick's Day parades start marching.

It's such a change from our quiet home in the mountains, where the snow is deep and the nights are early, where we're often settled in reading by dark. In New Orleans, we walk late at night, we walk all day. We visit the museum with the stunning and moving exhibits of the hurricane; as we did in St. Paul, we tour the Mississippi on a riverboat. We line up at the small, dark and crowded Preservation Hall for jazz and the simple sense of absorbing history and the rhythms of thousands who've been here before us. Some days we go separate ways: Dan to the war museum and me to a Louisiana cooking school. We take the streetcar to a jazz festival and explore cemeteries and parks. The city is still recovering from Hurricane Katrina. We don't prey on people for their stories, but we are good listeners who can sit on a park bench and listen if stories are offered. We're both singers, and join in when a street corner singer beckons us. As a crowd forms, we transform into a street choir and, in that moment, crooning and harmonizing with those songs, those spirituals, we are lifted and strengthened and ready to go back home.

——

Judy seems to be stable, and Mum has settled in.

"I was in a play yesterday," Mum says over the phone.

She's sitting in her suite at The Wellington, her cat ensconced on the window ledge, both of them looking out over the tops of budding trees and the Mississippi River Valley. I'm on my back deck in British Columbia where I can hear the distant rumble of the Little Slocan River. It's Easter weekend, and our first consecutive three days of lovely weather. Soon the daffodils will dare to blossom at the end of this endless winter.

"Wow, Mum, that's great! What was it about?"

"It was set in a salon. A beauty salon."

"Yeah?"

Mum owned and ran three Merle Norman studios for decades, so she knows the cosmetics business well.

"Yeah, well there were three customers, and some of them weren't happy, and they were giving the staff hell."

"Were you staff?"

"No, I chose the role of bitchy customer. I know just how they carry on. It was fun."

"Did you write the play?"

"No, someone else did. And one of the girls here, the activities director, got it all organized." Normally I object to the use of the term *girls*, but when you're ninety-two, you can say what you like.

"Did you memorize your lines, or did people use scripts?"

"Well some did. And some have voices so soft, they just can't project. They had to turn the acoustics way up."

I will never get over how my mother nearly died, survived

two heart surgeries, moved from her home, and now is walking, laughing and acting.

"Watch out, Betty White," I say.

———

The summer is so normal, a breather, a respite. Plant the garden, swim at the swimming hole, work various jobs. We're down to the final touches on *The Third Crop*, and I work long hours each day with the designer and editor, the proofreader and publicist. It's crazy, fast, skilled and wonderful. I am in my element, my most competent, most thrilled self. We plan the book launch party for mid-August at the Vallican Whole, where we expect several hundred people to attend. A week after that, the Whole will celebrate its fortieth year. It's a summer of guests and pot-lucks and good long visits. The sky isn't falling, and the shoe isn't dropping.

My book launch is fantastic, with old-time music and every part of our community attending; all the cultures, all the families new and old, friends from near and far. There's dancing and food and great stories. The Vallican Whole reunion is wonderful, with dancing and poetry, a pig roast and rock and roll, and a loud and raucous fundraising auction. It's all a homecoming. We're in our home community, satiated and happy.

Then the shoe drops, the sky falls.

———

We think our lives are divided into sections by births and deaths, world events, big moves or changes in jobs.

But our lives are fractured by phone calls. The call in the middle of the night, the shattered voice leaving a message, the phone that isn't answered.

"Honey, there's been a terrible plane crash."

Or

"I think it's time you all come."

Or

The phone that keeps ringing and ringing and no one answers.

⸺

I phoned Judy to tell her about all the great events of August, but she didn't answer. She had to go back in, David said when I reached him, and we all knew "in" meant the hospital. During the last round of treatment in July, they'd drained fifteen pounds of fluids from her and she'd been vomiting blood. I thought she'd done well after that, but perhaps I knew nothing. Perhaps she let me have my August celebrations without worry, as she always did for her wedding guests. Don't spoil the party.

David said they were meeting with doctors, to talk about shifting the focus to keeping her comfortable. These words are meant to comfort: an image of big fluffy pillows, a luxurious stolen day in bed reading books; words that sheathe the truth.

There is reference to "maybe six to eight weeks to live."

This dreaded day in our family has arrived.

My neighbours are heading to Spokane in the morning and offer a ride to the airport, but I need the weekend to get ready and there's time. I may be gone awhile. But I'm not sure; there's something too wrong with all this, and so I call Terry, Judy's stepson, the doctor who helped when Mum was in trouble. It's very late at night in Minnesota, but I have to know right away what to do.

"I wouldn't wait," he says.

Then begins the usual scramble: late-night packing, phone calls, emails, arrangements. Dan hits the computer to find a flight, and my friends deliver me to Spokane in the morning.

At the airports en route to St. Paul, I prepare myself. I can fall apart, or I can be strong. Numb and strong: for Judy, for David, for my mother. For myself. This is a time for resolve and strength and, during a crisis, our family can summon resolve and strength in spades.

David picks me up. We drive the tree-lined river route instead of the freeway and it gives us time to talk. Neither he nor I believe for a minute that Judy has six to eight weeks to live. Someone made that up to soothe us; it's a press release from a politician in trouble. And when we walk down the long hospital corridors and into her room, I know there is little time left. She knows it, too, and amid tears, laughter and back rubs, we get down to work. There are only a few words said: "I wish you had a few more days, Jude." And her simple answer: "So do I."

In Judy's office just off the big kitchen, her computer screen-saver is a picture of the three of us—her, Dan and me—huddled in rain gear on a whaleboat on the Bay of Fundy, grinning ear to ear and eating lobster sandwiches. It's been on her computer for eight years since we visited Andy and Chris in Nova Scotia. Judy wears new sunglasses, and is beautiful, trimmed down to petite, her hair black and her olive skin taking on colour fast in the ocean wind and spring sun after a long Minnesota winter.

That was the spring after her son and our father died within seven months of each other. That spring we rebuilt ourselves, with laughter and lobster sandwiches, and for years afterward on her computer, that picture of Dan, Judy and me, huge sandwiches and huger smiles, greeted her every morning. It greets me now, before I return to her at the hospital.

David and Amber, with her nursing skills, and Terry the doctor, meet with Judy and her medical team again and figure out how this will go: how she will be released in time for her to die at home. Judy asks us to pick up Mum at The Wellington and bring her to the hospital so they can talk privately before it all gets underway.

Mum is stoic, devastated.

Donna and her family make their last visit; a family conference is arranged with Judy chairing it from her bed; a meeting with her attorney; an arrangement for transport.

At some point in all this discussion and direction, she looked up and said in a bemused and kind way, as if offering a beatitude: "At least Rita will get a story out of this."

And then she signs more papers. She has made certain decisions and now she will act upon them.

This is Judy, grace, laughter, sorrow, steel.

———

We have made our final list together, our last great act as sisters.

Make a list, Judy would say.

Figure it out.

Have fun.

You can do it.

Judy made her lists on white notepaper, with a medium felt-tipped pen.

- American Fish Company—50 pounds prawns
- 10 large cans chicken broth
- 5 large tubs sour cream
- wild rice
- linens

Or for Mum's chores she wrote:

- Mom's cat to vet
- B-12 shots
- Menards—light bulbs

Judy's lists stayed neat or were rewritten.

I write my lists on a third of a sheet of 8½ by 11 paper, cut in threes the short way. I use a fine-tipped ink pen that won't smear in the rain or snow as I shove the list in and out of my coat pocket. On the top are chores to be done en route to Nelson and on the bottom are chores for on the way out.

So:

- Credit Union
- gas
- recycling
- Maglio's for TSP and furnace filters
- Then groceries and drug store and library

And on the way home:

- Farmer's Supply for blood and bone meal and black oil seed

My lists start out neat and become a scribbled-over mess with items written sideways, addresses for dropping things off or picking up, phone numbers.

When in doubt or struggling, make a list.

We made lists together sometimes:

- Live Met Opera Saturday—call Marlys

We made a list for the food for Dad's funeral long ago, when we struggled over what to cook, and struck upon all his favourites, even though they weren't on the regular menu at Judy's catering business. We talked to Mum and remembered everything Dad liked best, even the things he stole from the bulk bins when he got Alzheimer's, like butterscotch candies and peanuts in the shell. And our list read:

- Sliced tomatoes
- Cucumbers in white vinegar with pepper
- Baked beans
- Roast pork
- Mashed potatoes
- Coleslaw
- Apple pie with cold strong cheddar

When Judy and I drove together to North Carolina to pick up Dan at art school, we took:

- Binoculars
- Maps
- Bathing suits
- Books
- Wine carrier and glasses

Or when we took Mum to the Mayo Clinic:

For Mum:

- Books
- Housecoat
- Slippers
- Glasses
- Teeth

For Judy:

- Housecoat
- Remodulin and tubing
- Instructions for the heart pump

For Rita:

- Wine

And then that day in September, as Judy lay in her hospital bed, I rubbed her back with my left hand, and wrote down her requests with my right, sometimes had to lean down to hear her words muffled by the pillow as I wrote out her final list:

She said:

- Leave my wedding ring on
- Engagement ring in top drawer—if they can put it on
- Call the funeral home now
- Find the green porcelain necklace from Denise—in the jewellery drawer in long credenza

"What do you want to wear, Jude?"

"My black top and long-sleeved black jacket and matching pants (they're used to seeing me in black).

"Later, Denise can help take my clothes away to the Women of Nations, or the place where women need good clothes for job interviews, or the Goodwill."

- Open casket if appropriate (David decides)
- Ask Al Franken to say a few words at the wake
- Get Chris Coleman or Mike Faricy to bagpipe at the cemetery
- Kristi to play the violin
- Ask the mayor to say a few words
- Andy to officiate at the graveside—no religion

- Rita to speak for the Moirs
- David for the McLaughlins
- Heidi, Denise and Carol for the friends
- Ask Trish Hampl to read a poem
- Tell people to keep the speeches short and get to the bar
- Let the friends be in charge; you can't stop them anyway

Now take me home to die.

You've got your list.

You can do it.

—

The transport is made late at night. They carry her up the big stone front steps of her home on Summit Avenue, through the foyer and up the wide grand staircase where the wedding parties are always photographed, and into her bedroom.

We take turns sitting with her up on her large bed. Sometimes Mum crawls in with her. A last call is made to Brian in Winnipeg. Andy has arrived from Nova Scotia. The extended family—maybe a dozen or more of us—sleeps or stays awake and exhausted throughout Judy's house. She sleeps, semi-conscious, and then sits up in the middle of the night and starts talking, asking about arrangements; word spreads throughout the house and visiting begins again.

Someone orders pizza, and downstairs we eat and work

on her obituary, sending an emissary up to check out details with her. She continues to make choices. Cass holds up clothes so she can select the right black outfit. We get her engagement ring on with some effort. By morning she is barely conscious, but when some of her friends visit, their laughter and stories buoy her and their presence brings her comfort and completion.

The pain increases. Her breathing grows ragged. The family medical team works with her pain levels and all the other medical attention she needs until finally they ask everyone to leave the room while they remove the Remodulin pump that keeps her heart beating when all the rest of her body is trying to shut down. When the pump is removed she has several hours to live, and is unconscious.

At 11:45 p.m. on Labour Day, as the cathedral bells ring, Judy takes her last breath: on her king-sized bed, we say good-bye to our small and depleted queen.

—

Andy organizes the photographs into the slide show for Judy's wake and the reception. At her computer he sorts through a lifetime of pictures: hundreds of photos of babies and political campaigns and celebrations.

Her own childhood, six-year-old girl inside a picket fence in Winnipeg, at our father's childhood home on Toronto Street; black and white Judy, in tall socks, wool overcoat, beret. Then Judy through high school, earnest, smart. There is one photo of her in a cashmere sweater, her eyes dark; she is voluptuous, a young woman so full. Then Judy increasing, Judy with husband, Judy with two children and seven stepchildren. Then Judy without husband, without father, without stepson, without second son. Then Judy at first son's wedding, then Judy decreasing, Judy gone.

Like a childhood game we played making "movies," riffling a pile of recipe cards where the character drawn at the edge of each card dances until the movie is over.

Imagine Andy, at the computer, compiling Judy's life, until, at the end, we see her arm in arm with our mother, the two petite matriarchs, walking away from the camera.

⎯⎯

Judy has been dead for four days and we are in the interregnum, the down time when the funeral is planned, the obituary published, the speakers lined up, Judy's clothes delivered to the funeral home. David carries on, catering and hosting two large weddings at Summit Manor. Of course he doesn't bail out on them; as Judy did not cancel weddings after her son William's death, David does not cancel weddings after his mother's. It's as if Judy timed her death after one set of weddings and her funeral to follow after the next set. Anyone with a family business catering to other people's celebrations knows this, how you carry on even when your own life has been gutted.

The wake and burial are set for the Sunday and Monday after the weddings, and we are a stunning team. David preparing food, the large family and community of friends supporting each other, speakers writing their speeches, Mum the pillar of strength, Andy and I tackling the carriage house in the final purge.

Judy owned the carriage house that our folks lived in, but it has sat empty the seven months since Mum moved to The Wellington. Judy had tried to finish clearing it out after Mum left, but she didn't have the stamina.

Andy emerges from the slanted cupboard under the overhang in Mum and Dad's second-floor bedroom. It's a perfect place for hidden treasure, but what we find isn't treasure; rather, it's stored items long forgotten, that have caught and absorbed water and rotted from the leaks in the old tile roof.

Andy's dark hair is grey with cobwebs. He would look funny if we were all here together and could laugh at our situation, but it's not funny like when we did this with Judy. We're alone together and our spirits are so low. Andy is exhausted. He hefts out boxes of mouldy texts, some with a blue furry growth an inch thick. Dad stored these botany texts decades ago, all the precious cargo of his education.

There are moments of laughter, but mostly it's grim resolve and no tears. Not for Judy, not in this moment, and no nostalgia for this home our parents left behind.

Mum returns from The Wellington one day to help sort books. There are hundreds of them, maybe five hundred. She sits in the debris of her veranda, wedged into her chesterfield on the foot of space between stacks of books and CDs and magazines, and begins to sort.

"Rita!" I hear from the kitchen where I kneel, shoulders deep in a cupboard of mismatched pots and lids. "What?" I holler and then, knowing she can't hear me, limp stiff and crotchety, then straighten up and paste on a smile.

"Did you ever read this one by James Carroll?" she asks, then tells me something about him, the book, when she first read it.

"No, but it sounds really interesting. Maybe I'll take it home with me."

Back in the kitchen with my head and shoulders wedged back in the cupboard, I hear, "Rita?"

"Yes?"

"Here's this one about the Kennedys. Come see."

Oh dear god.

"Maybe you'd like it?"

Beside her are dozens of books about the Kennedys.

It goes like this, book by book, so hard for her not to turn each one over and examine it as some collectors would fine china.

We are doomed at this rate. And it's too hard on Mum to be back in her old home, now in such a mess as we rip the life out of it.

The next day when she's supposed to come back, we arrange instead for Judy's stepdaughter Carol to visit Mum at The Wellington with her small dogs. Mum needs this change, this liveliness, and we need her out of here so we can make the hard decisions she wants us to make because she can't make them herself.

Mostly, I can't look at what Andy is doing. I'm as much a packrat as my parents, especially about paper. I ask Andy to put all family papers aside for me to sort later. It will be a brutal process, but we know that in the midst of old newspaper clippings, there could be a family passport or birth certificate. There are boxes full of newspapers about the plane crash that killed William, brochures of Judy's run for political office in the same boxes with decades-old copies of *Life* magazine from the Kennedy assassination and the election of Pierre Trudeau and stories about Tommy Douglas. Boxes of papers that have been carried between Canada and the US for decades, from Manitoba to Minnesota, back to Manitoba, to Massachusetts and back to Manitoba and then again to Minnesota to end their storied lives. These caved-in boxes hold the history of my parents' political and family world.

I agree with Andy that we can't even look at the mouldy books. We load them onto the chair lift and the old boxes take their final humming ride downward to the garage door. I've salvaged anything my dad wrote, any bound theses or papers, but the discards out in the garage now rest, spines up, amidst heavy old TVs and broken lamps. In spite of myself, I look at them, consider trying to save some, clean them up for a botanist friend. But it's too sad, too late. Dad, I'm sorry, I really am. I'm not sure who you saved these for, maybe just couldn't let go; all these writers represented an intelligence you respected. Years of exploring and documenting; the texts' names sound dry, but I have to write them down, have to save something of them: *An Introduction to the Embryology of Angiosperms* by P. Maheshwari, *Atlas of Plant Morphology* by Emma Fisk and W.F. Millington, *Anatomy of Seed Plants* by Katherine Esau. But because you were a botanist, Dad, and I know your travels, I know what's behind each of these books. Painstaking journeys in the heat or cold of northern Manitoba or northwestern North Dakota, then long days with eyes to the microscope, lectures in little towns where only seven people show up to hear you speak about the land where they live. These authors may have been your friends, your colleagues, your idols or your students, and now we can't keep them for you anymore.

Two days later, a friend pulls up to the garage with his trailer. We load it for the recycler, the dump: a rotted carpet, broken fans, Dad's ruined books.

Months later, my chest constricts at the memory, as if the spores from all those texts remained in my lungs, and perhaps they did.

—

The night before Judy's wake, her neighbour Trish Hampl and I stood in the dark in Maiden Lane. We'd had a glass of wine with friends, and walked the block home down the broken and un-even cobblestones. The old streetlights softened the night and neither of us wanted to go back inside.

Trish and I see each other rarely, only on my visits to Judy, and then, though we are both writers and have that in common,

I am still Judy's sister, and that's the only reason I would have met Trish. Our visits always included Judy, and I'm not sure I know what to say on my own. They are both such gifted conversationalists, could smooth the edges off a broken brick just by the flow of their words.

There is some awkward shyness on my part in talking to Trish one-to-one, except that Judy is the topic of conversation, and we turn naturally to the details of her funeral. The reception after the burial will take place in Judy's home, in the room where she catered thousands of weddings, political fundraisers and family parties. We wonder what it will be like to attend an occasion at Judy's without her there.

We try to distill the essence of Judy, why she was the centre, the gravitational pull.

It wasn't just that she was a good cook; it wasn't just that she was at ease preparing for hundreds of people to come through her door. She offered hospitality, true hospitality. And as Trish and I stand in the soft light on the cobblestones worn out by decades of horses and carriages, in the lane amidst the carriage houses and the old mansions, this notion of hospitality turns to its meaning a century ago, when as a host you opened your home to strangers and stabled their horses. You offered not just food, but protection, the power of your standing in the community, your authority, your right to offer safe haven. It seems appropriate that as writers we talked about those old meanings: of host and hospitality, hotel and hostel, hospice and hospital, all those words from the same root, whether they bore religious or secular meaning.

Judy offered hospitality, not as in "hospitality industry" but because somewhere deep down she knew how to bring people together, with the power of her personality, her standing, her thoughtfulness and action; she offered a place for people to gather and talk things out, spark with laughter and ideas and then make something happen.

We talk about the poem Trish will read at Judy's graveside, and the food David will cook for her funeral. He'll prepare the food Judy loved: prawns, garlic mashed potatoes, roast beef in hot juices and an array of salads. Friends and family will bring sweets, or the potluck favourite they always used to bring to Judy's. David is now the one offering hospitality, a place for us to gather and eat and feel both protection and the generosity and strength of our spirits gathered together.

——

Her wake is September 11; September 12 her funeral and burial.

The coffin is open. There are just a few family members present right now. Depending on how she looks, depending on whether she is too discoloured from her death, David—as she requested—is to decide whether her coffin should be open or closed. It is his decision to make, but as in everything we are doing, we work together.

Her hands are dark, almost purple, but oddly, there is some peace in her hands. For once they are not swollen, and her nails have been taken care of beautifully. She's wearing the clothes she wanted, black, with the necklace Denise gave her. Her engagement and wedding rings are on. She's our Judy, as we always called her, "that's our Judy" whenever she did something remarkable. She looks like our Judy, although her mouth isn't right, and her large glasses mask her closed eyes.

Glasses off or on, we confer. Off, we agree: so people will look at her eyes.

In the St. Paul Irish tradition, the wake is held at the funeral home. At the funerals I've attended at O'Halloran and Murphy, the family forms a receiving line and guests arrive to view the body in an open coffin or pay respects at a closed coffin, depending on the circumstances and the family's decision. People visit, mourn and of course, laugh and carry forward. Judy's wake is on the tenth anniversary of 9/11, the September 11, 2001, attack on the Twin Towers in New York and the Pentagon. Politicians arriving have already spoken at commemorations; people have been reliving that trauma all day.

Mum stands with us to greet the hundreds who arrive: close friends and neighbours, co-workers from Judy's days long ago at the Legislature, staff from Summit Manor, and all the women Judy and Mum swam with at the nearby YWCA—the Ladies of the Pool.

Mayor Chris Coleman, Governor Mark Dayton, and US Senators Amy Klobuchar and Al Franken arrive. All are Democrats; all have looked to Judy for support; all have received the occasional sharp words of reprimand along with advice. If they weren't liberal enough, if they went off track, if they lost their nerve or didn't show up where they should have showed up. They've all shown up today; not for a few moments to put in an appearance and leave, but to stay and grieve and support our family and community. To mourn, and of course to laugh.

Al Franken, as Judy requested, says a few words.

He turns from the crowd to the coffin, to address Judy directly, and I love him for this. I wish someone had taped his speech, but we didn't. What I remember is how short he was, how solid. How absolutely right to talk to her sometimes then turn back to us. How he made us cry and then he made us laugh. How he talked about Judy's intelligence. "It's not always all about heart," he said. "It's also about brain; what we think and how we analyze."

And then he recalled the fundraiser she threw for him, but couldn't remember what she cooked. He asked: "Do you remember, David?"

David, surrounded by friends and family, hesitated, and I wondered if he could remember, could even respond, and then in his wonderful smiling David way he said, on just the right beat: "She said to clean out the freezer!" Al Franken erupted in laughter, and god knows Judy would have laughed out loud if she could.

—

That night after the wake, Andy watches TV way up on the third floor of Judy's house. He's officiating at the graveside in the morning and is trying hard to keep himself on some kind of emotional leash. We are a family of Calvinists; we are best with jobs to do, words to shape, emotions to forge into strength.

Andy and I look to each other, say hello, then I flop down on the big green chesterfield with him and stare at the huge TV screen. He clicks through all the news channels, all the 9/11 anniversary coverage of airplanes spearing the towers, the smoke and collapse, the people running in horror. We can't bear any more emotion today.

Andy stumbles onto a show about people fishing in muddy waters of the south and, in stunned fascination, we stare for an hour at *Hillbilly Handfishin'*. There is nothing more comforting or stupid than watching this show that we've never even heard of in Canada. A mother-daughter team and two young metrosexuals are covered in muck as they reach deep into fish caves in muddy Oklahoma waters, snagging monstrous catfish with their bare hands. They are so scared and so triumphant; they laugh so hard they fall down in the water, and cheer for each other as the commentator declares, redundantly, "José is elated with joy."

⸺

The coffin is heavy as we load her into the hearse, but we take turns, men and women carrying her. Traditionally, the men do this, but we are carrying Judy, and we all want to bear her.

We have chosen the pallbearers to reflect who she chose in her life: women and men, family and neighbours.

The hearse leads a procession down Summit Avenue, beneath the oak and maple in their fall glory. It slows as we pass Summit Manor, and then we cross the bridge to the State Legislature where she worked, then on to Oakland Cemetery. The day is crisp and sunny. The crowd waits, and we unload the coffin to the bagpipe's lament. When Mum is seated and Judy's coffin is in place over the grave, we begin.

Andy officiates, marshals our Scottish heritage to keep himself together.

Then Trish Hampl, elegant, composed, steps forward to read from her eulogy, a last letter to a friend who has died.

> *I'll keep describing things, getting the colors*
> *right, taking down the dialogue, packing*
> *the report with metaphor so it's art,*
> *watching the world be unlikely and eccentric.*
> *I call it honesty, as you do. But today*
> *I call it keeping you alive just a little longer,*
> *using the present tense though that's dishonest now,*
> *and it is unholy, darling, to hold you*
> *a second longer than you held on to us.*

David speaks for the family. The coffin before him is covered in red roses. There is no religion, just us, wretched, blessed, stoic; some faces ravaged with grief; others beatified with love and grace.

David's friends stand as honour guard beneath the massive trees as Judy is laid in the ground between her son William and our father. Mum watches as the unnatural order continues in its own sweet way, obeying no human laws or wishes; she sees her daughter buried next to her grandson. Dad is there, too, though, and even if we don't believe in the afterlife, there is some consolation in knowing they are in this final spot together on earth.

Mum rises from her chair at the graveside. "Well," she says. And we know it's time to take our next steps. She takes the arms of those around her, and she, our matriarch, our Consolotrix Afflictorum, leads us away.

——

"Now we'll do the corpse pose," says Eliza, our yoga instructor at the seniors' lodge back in BC.

The words startle me.

How can I not see Judy over and over, her final minutes, the moments when all of us gathered from our own fitful sleep, from throughout her big house; mother, son, brother, sister, all the large extended family, when we circled her, lights down, not touching, willing her to end her exhaustion, and ours.

We all saw her final moments, and the image plays and replays, Amber on her knees up on the king-sized bed with Judy, saying there's a lot of fluid coming out of her mouth, a lot; someone please get a towel.

How we all stayed with Judy, a final touch, a whisper of love, a prayer, and then getting out the list the hospital gave us, with the order of who to call: the police non-emergency number, so squad members can come to examine her; then the coroner's office, who know this is a home death, and who will then call the mortuary, who are waiting for this call and will come to retrieve the body.

How can I hear "corpse," "deep breaths," "let go" and not think of Judy's last breaths?

How can I lie on the warm floor of the seniors' lodge, in the corpse pose, looking up into the broad skylight, and not see us in two lines outside her bedroom, witnesses, honour guards flanking her removal.

⸺

I haven't had my own dog for many years, since Connor died at age sixteen in 1997. I'd never felt another dog stood a fair chance in comparison. Carly, who came with Dan into our relationship, died in 2006. We've been dogless for five years. It's two months after Judy's death and I long for life, for romping, for the sheer joy, messiness and busyness of a dog.

Dan and I visit the local animal shelters. Large German shepherds lunge at us against their pens. Posted descriptions warn: "Needs a firm hand. Needs fencing. Not good around children." If we attempt to walk them, they pull and leap on us. In our neighbourhood everyone walks dogs; most places are unfenced, and little kids ride by on bikes. We need a calm dog we can trust.

A small classified ad leaps at me: "Golden retriever puppies. Vet checked." Goldens may be ubiquitous everywhere else, but in my valley they are rare. We grew up with golden retrievers, along the banks of the Red River: recalling the plume of our dog's tail above tall grasses, or him pulling us all in a sled, in a harness made by our dad, makes me nostalgic and hopeful. They are our family dog: Dinty, who lived until age eighteen. Judy's dogs Sam, McDuff and McKinley and now David's Buchanan. We've always had male dogs: big protectors, big gentle goofs who love children, swimming, eating anything put in front of them, and who love the great outdoors. A dog that can carry a bird alive and drop it gently to fly off again. A dog that kids can crawl on, throw balls for, who will never nip or hurt.

"Dan?" I say. "What do you think?" And he, smart man, says: "Whatever you want."

The puppies are going quickly. There are a few males left and they won't reserve them. We drive an hour and a half north through the mountains and alongside glacial lakes to Nakusp, and then a further half-hour off to the southwest near to the ferry, on a day so wintry we normally wouldn't travel. What if there are only females left? Could I make that shift? Feminist though I am, to me dogs are male, and cats female. But what *if* there are only females left? En route, Dan and I talk it through; there are advantages: females are less likely to roam; they are loyal, smaller. Fearless, but maybe not so headstrong.

We pull into the ploughed driveway, where the breeder meets us and takes us into an attached garage, open to the big outdoors near the lake. The garage is large and clean, and back on a slight rise of land I can see the mother and father in their own enclosure. The breeder releases the puppies from their pens of fresh straw, and golden balls of fur with black noses bumble and tumble toward us. There are two sets of puppies, some seven weeks old and some eleven. The older puppies we're looking at are reduced in price because they're past the roly-poly stage, starting to get leggy.

I know dogs, like some people know horses. I kneel down and watch the puppies find me. There are three left, all female. One races to me, all over me, paws, mouth, licking and jumping. Another hangs far back. And one sits a few feet away, watches me, then approaches calmly, waiting her due and giving me mine. She sizes things up, and then she moves forward. I put my arms around her and hold her close. This is our dog, I say to Dan.

I realize she was born the week Judy died.

We name her Brier. Our cat's name is Lida Rose Chutney and the name Brier continues the rose theme. It's the name of the island across from my brother's in Nova Scotia, with its roaring winds and masses of wild roses. Brier: *Rosa canina*, the dog rose. The name reminds me of the Brier Cup, the bonspiel, and of my dad's curling trophies. The name Brier evokes the peaty smell of tobacco issuing from a brier pipe.

But mostly, Brier is a name we can call out loud through the neighbourhood, a good solid name full of music and rhythm.

As we drive home through a blizzard, see a car go off the road and the RCMP arrive, Brier is calm in her kennel and cries only once to be let out to pee. But when we are home, she goes into a kind of shock, and we can only think how she must feel at losing all her family. Outside, she runs and hides in the snow amidst bushes and we are lucky to find her. Inside again, she goes rigid and comatose under a table. We are at a loss; she won't be comforted, won't play. Then I look up to the chesterfield and see the stuffed toy puppy, small and golden, that a friend gave me a year ago. It's exactly the same colour and size as Brier, and I put it next to her. She relaxes, snuggles against it and falls asleep.

—

That first Christmas after Judy died, we were okay in our widely scattered family. It had been only three months and we were still high on being normal, carrying on, marching forward like Christian soldiers, though most of us weren't Christian and none of us were soldiers. But Christmas must be carried forward in our far-flung family posts—from British Columbia to Nova Scotia, Manitoba to Minnesota.

We are desperate to hold down the corner pegs of our family tent, as if without Judy as our Queen Pole, the ropes would rip loose and our entire family would fly into the sky, as if we could not withstand the tornado.

Far apart as we are geographically, we were—originally— all prairie people. We know how to repress our emotions and survive. We know how to put our arms straight to our sides, like

Irish dancers, press down with our palms as if pushing them toward the earth will hold in place whatever emotions would otherwise shriek their pain, rip us like the wind, shred us and blow us off the face of the planet. If we can stay solid, nail our emotions down like spikes, and keep to our traditions, our tent will hold.

In Canada, the three of us—Andy in Nova Scotia, me in BC and Brian in Winnipeg—are in our homes making the first attempt at rebuilding our lives. We are working at "rebuilding normal," at celebrating Christmas.

I enter upon a pre-Christmas frenzy of normalization: our Grassroots Grammas group sponsors a performance of *It's a Wonderful Life* at the Vallican Whole; Dan and I catch the community bus to Christmas by the Lake in Silverton; we bustle off to the Christmas Art Sale at the art school and the Winlaw craft fair at Winlaw Hall; we build a Solstice bonfire and play with our puppy and I bake shortbread by the thousands, skidding to a halt on Christmas Eve.

In Nova Scotia, on Christmas Eve, Andy and Chris eat lobster and tourtière; on Christmas Day they cook a turkey and invite friends over. In Winnipeg, Brian cooks a turkey and shares it with his cat, and here in our home in the Slocan Valley our table is full with turkey and friends, red wine and laughter.

At Judy's home in Minnesota, where every Christmas Eve for forty years she had cooked and served roast beef and all the trimmings, David and Amber serve roast beef and all the trimmings. As they had always done, the big extended family, including our mother, the matriarch, and a newborn in the family, trooped to Judy's big home on Summit Avenue, amidst all the other stately homes on the historic street.

It's so familiar, like Currier and Ives: fresh snow nestled onto the dark limbs of the massive oak and maple, softening their stark black branches; old streetlights muffling the light and even the sound.

On this Christmas after her death, the only sound would be the huffing breath of the parents carrying presents, and excited kids calling out, "Merry Christmas."

Inside Judy's old mansion, you might think it would be sedate, orderly. But on Christmas Eve all rules are thrown out. Adults play kazoos and kids eat too much candy and hundreds of pictures are taken to record the happiness of it all. Kids tear into packages beneath the big tree, and the family dogs paw off their reindeer antlers and skid through torn wrapping paper on the old parquet floors. There's laughter and drinks and the baby is passed around the circle of women. And then everyone says, *Well, we got through that okay; we did okay. We even had fun.*

On Christmas morning, we send pictures to each other—to Nova Scotia and Minnesota, Manitoba and British Columbia—of our Christmas trees and tourtière and roast beef and our presents and our dogs and cats wearing Santa hats and reindeer's antlers.

There is joy, truly, because we all love Christmas; Judy loved Christmas; and we love the snow and the tree and the glorious music we sing at the top of our voices. Christmas is corny and wondrous and filled with peals of bells and laughter.

And it is true, too, that sometimes in the midst of the highest, most pure Hallelujah there is quiet weeping. We keep on keeping on. We opt for joy at the same time as we remember, with the help of all our traditions and ceremonies. We remember the people we loved who have died, maybe a long time ago or maybe so recently we can barely speak of them without falling to pieces.

Dan and I attended our first Christmas Remembered at the United Church in Nelson. I sat quietly, sometimes convulsing with tears. And what brought me joy, the most uplifting joy, was the handbell ringers. I sat in awe and delight, crying and laughing all in the same moment. As the church bells had tolled the end of my sister's life, tonight they peal for the sheer joy of living.

Rosa Canina: 2012

I no longer stay for the last minutes of yoga class, though out of respect for me, our instructor refers to them as the "final relaxation" instead of "the corpse pose." Even "final relaxation" seems such a euphemism for "corpse pose" that it strikes me as funny as I write it out. In spite of her consideration, I still can't do it and slip out the door while others lie resting in peace.

But each session I learn something: today Eliza said, "Breathe out something you want to let go of," and my instant and honest answer, "Judy," shocked and surprised me as I exhaled deeply.

"Now breathe in something you want to bring into yourself," and my answer relieved me because again it was her name that flooded in.

I want to release the pain and anguish of her death, for her and me. I want her to re-enter as laughter and intense love, sun and wind and wisdom.

As Judy got sicker, she wouldn't let me see her feet because of the sores and swelling. Her winter boots were always unzipped at the side. Her fingers were always swollen and cold. In the end, she couldn't get rid of the fluid, no matter the medications, the drains the surgeons inserted to help siphon it off, the type of dialysis they performed regularly. Water accumulated around her tiny midriff like a tire, her belly like a football. Over the last decade she had lost weight gradually, going from heavy to trim, but when she became sick she went quickly from petite to minimal.

In the hospital before she died, as I massaged her back the skin moved across her shoulders, loose like a puppy's. Her skin was like doeskin, dark like suntan, from the drugs. Her skin was simply Judy's skin, her shoulders the shoulders I rubbed each night at her home over the years as she leaned forward at the kitchen table, tired at the end of a long day of cooking for hundreds of people, and said, "Just rub my neck for a minute."

⎯

In Israeli dance class at the school gym in Winlaw, near where I live, our teacher Haya asks why we're not smiling and laughing: "It's just a dance," she chides us with a smile for our seriousness. She reassures us that eventually we'll learn the intricate steps.

We dance hand in hand in a large circle. We step with the left foot when it should be the right. One of us starts off clockwise when we should move counter. We crash into each other; we concentrate on our feet, which, by the end of class, we can barely lift.

"It's okay," she says. "You can laugh!"

I want to be happy and lightfooted; it's eight months since Judy died, and I want to be magnificent, competent, ethereal. I want to rise above it all, but instead, I stumble. Young Annie, Québécoise and wiry and strong, sees me leave the room crying, and she comes to me—Annie who I don't even know—and she embraces me. She doesn't say anything, just holds me when I am crying and can't do the steps, when I feel stupid and clumsy.

Annie's embrace braced me, her young lean body mothering me, sistering me.

It will take time, that's all. Happiness doesn't come without giving grief equal footing. Years later I will be able to laugh at myself, but right now I am a grudging, grieving Calvinist and my steps are leaden; grief holds them to the ground. I need to let go. I know that. I will work at dancing toward lightness, but these steps are new to me.

Dan and I take Brier to her first obedience class. She wants to meet everyone and their dogs, to check out their treats and toys. She wants to climb onto people's laps. She is such a golden retriever.

She learns to sit on command for five seconds, or ten. We work with hand signals and voice together, or hand signals alone or voice alone. At home, I hide around a corner, stretch my arm into her line of sight and move my flat hand downward. I hear her lie down. I leave my hiding place and give her a treat. You're a good girl, Brier. You're our good girl.

In our family, we send emails back and forth. Andy and Chris bring home their new border collie puppy, Shep. We call Mum often. We talk about her life at The Wellington, from her exercise classes to the latest entertainment and the gossip in the dining room.

"What I like about this place is that no matter how bad things are in your own life, there's always someone worse off than you," Mum philosophizes. "And they've all been through this. When you get to this age, and if you've had children, almost certainly one of them has died. It doesn't take away the pain, but it eases it to know you're not alone."

Like my mother, I, too, exercise: but I know I am deliberately trying to outrun Sadness.

Sadness and I are on a track together, and on one round I lap him: I am light and run swiftly, pass him and laugh. The next day he overtakes me.

I begin my Outrunning Sadness List:

- Buy flowers in winter, and damn the expense.
- Clean up one space and make room for something new: a thought, a movement, a colour.
- Invite friends over at the last minute and whip up a feast.
- Wash the car. Wash the dog.
- Sit on a park bench and see who comes by.
- Take down from your wall all the reminders of dead people, even if you bring them back selectively.

- Make new friends: young friends. Their problems and joys will put your own life in perspective.
- Rethink all the condescending well-meaning things you've said to old people. You're becoming one.
- You are one.
- Read a good murder mystery. The deaths in them serve only to move the plot forward.

I know intellectually, and even feel sometimes, that my loss of memory, the craters left in my brain after Judy's death, my unexpected incompetence and clumsiness, will ease. The part of my brain that is always preoccupied with her will come back to earth and help me think straight again, engage and carry through.

I think of families who lose everyone in an accident, a war, and I rage at some facile commentator who—the next day—says the healing has begun and may take weeks, even months. It will take five years, or twenty years, or generations, before the story becomes whole again.

- Go make some soup.
- Go rescue something.
- Dance in your apron.
- Be strong for someone, even if you can't be for yourself.
- Listen to Connie Kaldor.

I told my mother I was trying to outrun sadness.

"The bad days come at you unbidden," she says, "and can take you over, but you have to choose joy and laughter. You simply have to opt for joy."

This month I have:

- Planted roses given to me by my eighty-seven-year-old neighbour
- Organized a house concert
- Met with friends to discuss a community problem and survived an ugly meeting
- Gone to a comedy show
- Organized the kitchen at a dance
- Put up a greenhouse
- Worked odd jobs
- Sent Mother's Day flowers a week early by mistake
- Hauled rocks and dug gardens
- Danced in my apron

This month I have lapped sadness. He stands behind the green of a spring larch as I—busy, laughing, panting—race by. I know he is there. One day we'll run together like old adversaries, respect and push each other forward, but for a moment I'm ahead, and he has the grace to allow me this gain.

——

In the forest, Brier jumps high like a kangaroo. Bounding and pouncing. She loves to sail over downed trees, leap high for the ball. She is a natural for agility training, where the dogs jump, run through tunnels, go up and down A-frames and teeter-totters.

But in agility class in the big open field, the instructor insists that the new young dogs take it slowly, with very low jumps. The point isn't to see how fast and high they can go at first, she tells all of us who are impatient to show off our dogs, to let them leap and twirl, but to make sure they learn happily and with success. It's all new to them, the staged jumps, the discipline, the strange objects like teeter-totters. You don't want injuries on their young bones, she says. You want to be in this for the long run. Brier watches the older dogs; I am sure she learns from them and wants to do what they do.

She is too young to learn the weave poles. A dog has to be at least a year old, when the growth plates in their bones have closed. Otherwise the rigourous weaving between poles, that flashiest showiest part of the agility trial, could harm her young and growing joints and spine.

Later, Brier, later for that.

———

Like my dog, I am impatient for joy. I want to forego this slow training in grief, waiting for my growth plates to harden.

Look at me, look at me! I want to shout to the world, I have triumphed!

I want to jump for joy. I want joy to hit me like grief did, like a baseball to the sternum, I want to reel against the washing machine, clutch the edge, double over gasping for joy.

I want explosions of laughter, marching bands parading down the back road, flower petals drifting from the clouds.

But mostly joy is slow to return: like moss on rocks, it takes its sweet time and the proper conditions.

The timelines of grief and joy: grief, so swift to hit. Joy, so slow, but so tenacious, like the wildflower growing in hard rocks.

Joy is all clichés, the small things: the dog tucking her legs to sail over a jump or braving the river current for the simple love of swimming.

Joy is hearing my mother's voice.

Joy is listening to Dan learn the clarinet, the notes deep and sweet, reverberating through my shoulders.

Joy is muscles straining to move one more rock into place, and next to it planting flax that will wave slender and blue, lightness and heaviness side by side.

———

In my new garden, grasses wave their inflorescence, such a lovely word. As I walk outside with my morning coffee, their slender stalks of flowers, seed heads, shimmer in the morning sun. I begin to learn about grasses; to see the world again through a botanist's eyes, my father's eyes, grasses wild or grasses cultivated. I attend a session on landscaping, and begin to imagine the heights and widths of plants, the seasons when they flower, variegations in leaves, wide or slender, white striped or solid, six feet tall or two. I learn that solid rocks anchor the gardens; that flax with its blue flowers or sage and grasses with their waving spires give breath and air, movement and light. I make a garden of rocks that represent each member of my immediate family, with my parents just slightly apart from my brothers and sisters. Brian's rock reminds me of a buffalo; he is solid and large and Manitoban. Judy is our leader with an upright rock. Mum is rounded and anchored, Dad the Scot more craggy and faceted.

My friend gives me seven flax plants, not knowing there are seven in my family, and I plant them near the seven rocks.

What are the depths of my sister that leave me aching at her loss? Her grace, though she was not graceful in the classic sense of the word. Her grace came from her ability to keep going under the most devastating of circumstances. Her strength, her way of making life secure for other people, her laughter when laughter seemed impossible. Her ability both to speak and to listen.

How often is that the case? How often do we leave a situation and realize that mostly we spoke and didn't listen, or that we listened and never got a chance to speak. How unsatisfying it was as a conversation, if it was supposed to be a conversation.

With Judy it was always listening and speaking. And at some point we would resolve the issue, or figure a way to set it aside for now, or to find its absurdity and laugh about it.

I miss the laughter alongside the gravity. I miss the blue flax by the rock.

From Dan's shop, I hear opera soaring from the boom box, the roar of the propane forge that heats the metal, and then the hammer on anvil. I love this. I love the fire, the soaring aria, the clanging and the sparks. Dan's forging garden gates. As I dig in the dirt, I know that the glowing metal, once pounded into shape, gets dipped in the quench tank, where the metal hisses as it cools and tempers and grows strong.

Everything's a metaphor these days: the forging, the tempering, the wind in the grasses. The young dog and her antics that lighten my spirit.

I know Brier is outside the shop with her ball and, just when it is most inconvenient, she'll run in to drop it in the quench tank, and that Dan will fish it out for her and toss the dripping ball out the shop door as far into the forest as possible. She'll leap and bound, and retrace its path. She'll run by the ball six times, practising how to track and smell, and just for the sheer joy of running. And then she'll pounce.

The words our dance teacher, Haya, uses are water flowing past my head. She tells us that one step, the Yemenite, is the same step we use in a different dance. The words sink in and make sense, translate through my brain, pool into place. I lock my eyes to her legs; her right leg moves forward, my right leg moves forward; her left swings sideways, so does mine. I cannot pay attention at the same time to the elegant movement of her arms;

I am an Irish dancer, hands still, only my legs matter now, linked to hers by rhythm, counting the beats, concentration.

Then I close my eyes and dance easily, don't watch the instructor or try to think. I just let go to the familiarity of the music and steps; grace notes earned, a newfound lightness granted because, no matter my mood or the weather, I kept on dancing.

⸺

In Winnipeg, Brian attends the Wellness Centre every day, where he walks and bikes for miles. In Nova Scotia, Andy hikes the paths behind his home on the Bay of Fundy. In St. Paul our ninety-three-year-old mother attends exercise class twice a day. At her annual post-operative heart checkup at the Mayo Clinic, she performs a can-can step to the joy of the astonished doctor.

We are trying so hard. We are getting there. It takes time. That's all. Time and effort. A person can become stuck in grief: I could become stuck in grief. The story of our family could become mired. We are trying, all of us, to push out of this bog.

Judy would hate for her story to be stuck; she would hate for us to be so sad, as hard as it is to get up and get moving.

Grief can seduce you in its chaos and exhaustion, because that too is a way to live, a way that becomes known and safe. In grief, you are asking, demanding, that people tread softly, or let you be. I could wear widow's weeds for too long, and Judy would hate that. "For God's sake, make a list," she'd say. "Get moving."

She knew grief more than most of us, and we were struck repeatedly by her grace. When her husband died, she finished raising her sons. When her stepson died, she and his mother held the family firm through his long slow death. When William died in the plane crash, she grieved hard, then regrouped and regathered and carried on.

I once stayed with her for five months. We lived our separate and conjoined lives, me on her third floor every winter morning looking out through the stark black branches and crenellated rooftops backlit by the deepest pink and orange sunrise over the Mississippi. I worked on a book while she worked in the kitchen two stories below, preparing for a wedding, setting up for a fundraiser, or doing her daily errands. Those winter afternoons I helped her, or spent time with Mum or my sister Donna.

I was Judy's right-hand woman in an easy way, never one-sided, but she was my lead and I danced so confidently to her rhythms. We led individual lives we each respected, either as a team in her home, or in our far separate homes half a continent apart: but as a duo we were indomitable.

The question I pose to myself is this: Do I have the same magnificence to carry on, to dance without my older sister in the lead?

—

The other day I got some feeling—maybe it was the sunshine, or in an unguarded moment when laughter erupted instead of tears—I had this split second where I felt that not only I, but

Judy herself, was getting past the initial shock of her death. And because I don't believe in afterlife, nor did she, I didn't know the source of this feeling, but simply, somehow, we conjured each other. There was simply a moment of communion; "It's okay. This is where we are and let's get on with it."

———

In our family we get new puppies; we buy new hats. Then David and Amber tell us they are expecting their first child.

———

It's September, a year since Judy's death. Dan and I leave Brier with friends and drive 2500 km cross-country and then south to Minnesota to pick up my mother, then drive back up north 750 km to Winnipeg to visit Brian. From there, Mum, Dan and I fly east to Nova Scotia.

Andy and his wife, Chris, live in the village of Freeport on the Bay of Fundy. After we rest a few days from our trip, they treat us to a whale-watching tour.

Our last trip out on this boat was nine years ago, with Judy, eating those big lobster sandwiches—the picture on her computer screen. God we were happy, even back then in our fresh grief for Dad and William. And now we're on the whale-boat again, striving for that same kind of happiness without her.

Chris has worked on the whale tours for years and is our professional guide. Andy's taken time off work, and our old friends Janice and Claudette from Halifax have joined us for this glorious day. On the boat, our mother, sitting snug in her rain gear and ball cap and wrapped in a blanket, tells our friends matter-of-factly that this is her last trip to Freeport. And though we are tempted to say, Oh no, we'll be out on this boat again next year, we are not so callous or so stupid as to pretend that is so. She is sharp, strong and healthy, but such long travels, the airports, car rides, the constant changes and ins and outs and ups and downs, are tiring, and I realize just how much her independence and sharpness rely on solid assistance and a daily routine.

Chris points out a flat empty spot on the ocean. A whale was here, she says, and we all go quiet.

She tells us that a whale leaves a footprint, a flat space when it goes under. The smooth water the size of a whale rests quietly, surrounded by waves and ripples. It amazes us, this stillness where once there was the absolute stunning power and grace of forty tons of whale leaping from the water.

A large poster taped to the cabin illustrates marine life in the Bay of Fundy. The rare and endangered right whale, the huge humpback, the finback or fin, the smaller minke, the porpoises and dolphins.

We see a bright orange and black puffin, a lighthouse, many rocks and birds, but except for the footprint, we see no sign of whales. It doesn't matter: it's a stunning day and as the captain steams out to deeper waters, we take dozens of pictures of Mum, with Andy, with our visiting friends, and we pepper Chris with dumb questions. We try to match wits with the visitor who once asked, while on the Atlantic Ocean, how far they were above sea level. Do whales lay eggs, I ask, trying for a straight face, but can't manage.

Our silliness, our wish to be silly even, is such a joy. All of us together on this boat, leaning into ocean spray, posing for pictures, bundled in blankets, helping ourselves to hot chocolate.

Far off a geyser erupts and someone shouts, "There's one!" We are whale spotters, as in days of the old whaling boats, and the excitement must be similar: Thar she blows! Out there, out there! Whale at three o'clock, Chris tells the captain while grabbing her binoculars. The captain changes course and from then on that's how our day goes, shouts and excitement and stunned reverent silence when we drift and watch. From that moment we see whales everywhere, all the kinds possible. We are in the magic zone where the animals present themselves to us, as if we've paid enough attention, worked hard enough, need them enough, care enough, and need this one perfect day that will last us the rest of our lives. As if the ocean has opened to us, and we to it, as if the first whale's footprint has opened the veil between them and us.

Far away we spot two geysers close together. A right whale, Chris says quietly, and quickly speaks to the captain. She turns to us: only the right whale has a split blowhole, so the spray blows in two streams, like a *V*. The right whale is endangered and rarely seen, she says. There are only four hundred in the world. We are awed and silenced: this trip is an extreme privilege.

We've seen a fin whale, which Chris explains is the second-largest species in the world at up to eighty-two feet, second only to the blue whale. We've seen breaching humpbacks, a mother and juvenile leaping high into the air one after another. Most of us are too dumbfounded to get a proper picture, or simply lay our cameras against our chests and drink the scene into our memories.

We are satiated, complete, sapped, like religious pilgrims who have witnessed their miracle. When we steam back toward shore, first the porpoises in their dozens and then the dolphins in their hundreds leap alongside of us; and even Chris, who has done this job for a decade, whoops with glee. "I've never seen so many!" she calls out to us. "Never! There must be four hundred dolphins!" And they leap and play and laugh as my mother curls up in her blanket, a hot chocolate in hand, and watches her host of angels. If this is her last trip to Nova Scotia, if she does need to be danced attendance, then what better than this?

——

The next day, we receive the phone call. David and Amber's baby has been born. They name him William. We cheer and laugh and whoop and holler. A child is born.

——

Mum returns to St. Paul from the Nova Scotia trip more at peace than before. She has seen both her sons in their lives in Canada and feels satisfied and complete. And now there will be another sense of completion. At a ceremony dedicating a plaque to Judy in the park near her home in St. Paul, David and Amber arrive pushing a baby carriage, and Mum lifts her great-grandson, William, into her arms.

In the midst of celebration and speeches about Judy and her work on the park, in the midst of rebirth in our family, I remember the ocean's still water, the footprint where once there was such power.

—

You keep saying to yourself, okay, enough with Death. Stop commemorating it. But funny how Death demands an anniversary, as do marriages and births. It will take decades before the anniversary slips by unremembered: first anniversary of death, second, third, fifth, tenth; until the anniversaries smooth into your days like river rocks at the heart of the garden.

In 2003, when the memorial site in northern Minnesota, near Eveleth on the Iron Range, was dedicated on the first anniversary of the crash that killed her son and the senator, Judy drove us there. William had been dead a year, and Dad for five months.

William's untimely death changed our lives forever, is the jagged stone that sits deep in our hearts; the one we work to round and smooth. To cope with our losses we looked for signs, not of reason, but of beauty.

Hundreds of us walked in silence along a large circular path through a forest much like my own back home, pausing before monolithic stones carved for each of the six passengers who died.

The ancient stones on the circular path stand in tectonic tribute. Their carver, lead sculptor Phil Rickey, spent ten weeks talking with the victims' families and sitting with the ancient rocks until they spoke to him. Then he began his work.

William was just twenty-three; his monument stone is two billion years old. Shining, tall and powerful, chiselled edges not yet worn smooth, it rises amidst young slender fir dancing in the wind. Judy wept, we all did, but she smiled too, at the beauty.

When the plane crashed that snowy day, when it sheered the trees and hit the ground and all the people inside were killed, the first rescuers at the site said eagles soared overhead. It was eerie, they said. So quiet after the crash; quiet and beauty and eagles and devastation.

An Anishinaabe poet, LeAnn Littlewolf, who had worked with the senator, wrote "The Wellstone Poem." It's carved into a boulder even older than the others, the colour of jade, and stands sentry to the path through the forest. In the wind I stood with Judy and my family in silence as we read.

> *The eagles circle*
> *In a ceremony*
> *To guide their kind friends home.*
> *Though our time here is brief,*
> *An ancient truth circles with the eagles:*
> *That spirits never die.*
> *They stay alive*

In love, in hope,
In eagles' wings touching the sky,
In people extending hands to one another
To circle like an eagle
And bring everyone home.

Judy is gone now, and in 2012 at the ten-year anniversary of the crash, she, too, was remembered. Buses and cars full of people travelled through the snow to the memorial site. There were miners and Indigenous singers and poets, children and families and the politicians who loved and worked with those who died.

I'd always hoped to be there with Judy, to stand at William's stone as she faced her own death. I had hoped she would live that long.

David and Amber were there with their newborn son, William. David said it was so eerie, how the eagles came to the site again, six eagles this time, an eagle for each passenger. And even if you don't believe in such things, he said, it's strange, isn't it, and sends a shiver through you. It was cold, he said, but one of those really beautiful snowfalls started during the ceremony, the kind that makes everything a little softer and quieter.

——

Just before Solstice in December, I spring an idea on Dan. "Let's have a party," I say. "I know the time frame's short."

"All right," Dan says, sensing my need to regain my old verve, my ability to whip together a big party on short notice.

"Let's have a bonfire. Let's celebrate Solstice with hot dogs and kids and neighbours."

"When's Solstice?"

"December 22. Saturday."

"That's in three days."

"Yeah. Just listen."

"Okay."

"Let's put up more Christmas lights."

"Which tree would we put the lights on?"

"The one near the fire pit."

"We'd need an extension cord."

"We have lots. And all those lights."

"We'd need a ladder."

"Yes."

"Okay," he says, done stalling and instead getting into the spirit, "I could build a bonfire."

"Yes."

"We could ask everyone to bring wood."

"We'll invite all the neighbours," I say. "We'll invite Mireille and Monique, Marcia and Moe and Madeleine, Sophia and Sarah, Shauna and Sherallyn and Sierra."

"What about Craig?"

"Craig and Christophe, Micha and Mat, Mark and Marco. And Mark who lives with Martine."

"Rod?"

"Rod and Ron, Don, Dale and Dan. And the little kids with old names: Oliver and Charlotte, Makala and Immanuel, Evan and Alma and the little girl named Scotti, and teenaged Marco who's in plays. And adults with old and beautiful names: Rafaella, Tamara, Uta, June and Freya, Lydia and Lisa and Lois."

"More *s*'s," I say, by now talking to myself as well as to Dan.

"Yes!" I answer myself, on such a lovely alliterative roll that I am laughing. "Shirley and Stan, Seamus and Steph and Sharon. And those with French names: Gaetan, Leo and Emilée, and the reliable names of reliable friends like Ed and Paul and Barb."

The firewood arrives in the afternoon, Mireille pulling a trailer behind her four-wheeler that she and June unload. Steph wheelbarrows larch from his woodshed next door. Others drop off cardboard boxes full of split birch and fir, and Dan strings lights while I whittle hot dog sticks from the snow-covered branches of hazelnut.

We lay out candy canes and chocolates and hot apple juice, fried onions and potato chips, smokies and cheese dogs and turkey dogs and tofurkey dogs. And outside the real dogs play and chase each other, and leave the kids alone.

Around this fire, I watch the faces: Scotti, named for her father who died before she was born. Marco, shy teenager who recently took to acting; his first roles as a fork, a wolf and a villager. The men and women who drive trucks and work up north, home for the holidays or just ready to leave. The retired people, the little kids just starting school. The joyous and the grieving and the hopeful: we all watch the fire as the sparks rise high to the stars, to Sirius and Orion, and know that tomorrow the light will grow stronger.

STELLA MATUTINA: 2013

We have had our Solstice bonfires, winter potlucks, our story-telling festival, our celebrations. Now is the interregnum, when all we want is spring. The snow is not soft or quiet. There are no more Christmas tree lights lighting the night. Right now there is nothing. No project, no deadline, no jazz, no juice. The world outside is dead. Last week's hints of spring are snowed over and jagged with ice.

A neighbour hitchhiking to town, named Robin, how appropriate, remarked upon the cold.

"Cold?" I replied, thinking of my brother who is weathering a Nova Scotia storm, snowdrifts packed by 107 km winds, sculpted so hard they can't open the door. Cold? I can't talk about cold when my brother in Winnipeg sets foot into thirty-five-below temperatures and that's before the wind chill.

But Robin's right, winter here in the Slocan Valley has hit its past-due date and the desultory snow is a nuisance, a nasty dog that lunges out of sheer boredom.

I read in a mystery how the ruling of death by suicide, in the particular case being outlined, was questionable as the man was too short to reach the fixture from which he was hanging, and there was no chair or ladder nearby. Today, I find myself surveying light fixtures, for I, too, am short.

Today there is no Judy, where yesterday she was with me as I baked and peeled vegetables for a dinner I catered. Yesterday, as I fussed and worried, she said, or I conjured her to say, "We're in good shape." But we weren't really, and the dinner was only a moderate success. A February success. A "let's get it over with" type of accomplishment.

There's a song our choir is learning: "Hard Times Come Again No More." I love the old words, like "sup sorrow with the poor" or "frail forms fainting at the door." Love that old determination with words, hate it when good strong words like "wretch" are removed from songs, or prettified. There are times we are wretches, times we are wretched wretches or when we sup sorrow, not share it, but sup it, as if it were a hot soup searing our throats and finally hitting our bloodstream.

On this wretched February day, I sup sorrow with a fellowship of wretches.

Now, a year and a half after Judy's death, I am not as devastated as I was. I have "gotten on with life," written fine speeches, laughed hard, raised my voice in song, loved and am loved, train my dog and work out regularly on the treadmill.

But on these bleak wretched days of February, in the small moments when busyness is finished, when a list is completed and the next one not pressing, then Sorrow does come calling.

"Cold? No, no, we don't know cold here," I say to Robin. "Cold is somewhere else, in Manitoba and Nova Scotia." But this February cold, its greyness, is mean, too. A testing, a taunting, when your eyes flicker to the light fixture to measure the length of the rope.

———

Each night at 11:45 my heart lurches. It lasts a few minutes as I lie in bed, jerks me awake if I am asleep. Sometimes it happens at 9:45, which I attribute to the time difference between BC and Minnesota, or perhaps I make up the coincidence of hours.

Each night, unless I am so exhausted from physical work that I fall straight to sleep, I relive her death, her last minutes struggling and letting go.

And with it, I rip up my insides, silently, as Dan sleeps next to me, or reads, our backs or feet touching. I panic about choices, about happiness, about contentment, about safety and coziness and love, compared to a life of being single, its risks and commitment. At 11:45, I relive her death and I wonder what will be my summation at my own.

And I wonder if I have, in the face of the deaths in our family, the Alzheimer's, the brain tumour and the plane crash and now Judy, opted for food and wine and community potlucks and the same old safe jobs. As if anything more risky means untimely death, or losing all I have worked for, the yard with roses, the dog trained to lie down on command, the partner who vacuums and likes to read aloud to me, as do I to him.

Each night she dies again, and again and again.

This morning before waking, I dream I have gone to a therapist, and by some coincidence my brother Brian and my mother are with me; they're along for the ride, in Winnipeg, so they sit in on the appointment.

"Every night at 11:45 I relive her death," I tell the therapist. "Oh no, oh no," cries Mum, who hasn't known this, who cries out for me as much as for Judy. And Brian simply drops his head to his chest, and I know the same thing happens for him.

We are all choosing life; we are past—or I am, I hope—the thought of simply ending my own life because I couldn't live without her. Long ago I didn't believe it when people would declare that someone simply couldn't go on living without the person they loved, but now I understand. Thoughts of suicide are fleeting impulses, a quick note and then do it, before you can reconsider. But the dog barks, the dishes need washing; ordinary everyday chores demand their due.

——

We finally fence some of our property. Finally, wild roses grow unshorn by deer; on the roses' light pink petals, yellow pistils and stamens, bees rub their legs, delirious with pollen. Because of the deer fence, we can enjoy the Oregon grape, its brilliant yellow flowers tall with jagged leaves against the bulwark of fir. Tiny cedar fronds hug close to the shade of the forest floor. And arnica's furry green leaves await a single yellow flower. Daffodils, seven kinds, creams and oranges, yellow and white, turn their full faces to the sun.

Today I buy a petunia—silly name, with dark flowers; its black velvet blossoms will be my one nod to death. I tuck the plant into a riot of neon blue lithodorum, orange callies, spikes of maroon snapdragons and dancing grasses. The black flower signifies grace, the acceptance by Death itself that there is a season, and it will nestle and rest in my garden, taking its own vacation for the summer.

In her barnyard, our neighbour Tamara drives her tractor, "Buttercup," to the winter's pile of horse manure, shoves and swivels, lifts the full scoop of manure high above the frame on the back of our old Dodge Dakota. She dumps in three scoops and we head home down the dirt road.

I haven't left the property for four days, after running around madly for weeks and then getting sick. I rarely get sick or cancel appointments, but Dan and I are sneezing, coughing and rundown, so we stay home and tend to chores. All the boring wonderful routine: I paint the new gate while he heads to the forge to make hinges. Digging in the new flower beds, wandering, pondering, moving rocks. I hand-water the grass seed two to three times a day, hope the red dogwood whips will take hold in a big hole filled with a slush of compost and peat. I push the old wheelhoe, a contraption we grew up with and which now seems quaint, a relic, but which silently—with muscle and grace—moves through the garden leaving its quiet wake, accomplishing what a rototiller manages but without the noise and danger.

The dogs—ours and a neighbour's—race crazy loops around the garden, and if by chance Brier gets in, she digs a hole in the potato patch, buries her ball and tosses a seed potato in the air. I plant tomatoes and peppers in the greenhouse, heather and forget-me-nots and violets near the forest, lupins and columbines on small hillsides. All this bounty. All this hope.

Hummingbirds buzz the feeders; pine siskins and white-crowned sparrows bathe and fluff in the bird bath Judy sent me a decade ago. They've never used it until we enclosed this garden, set it in the shade beneath the Saskatoon bush full of white flowers.

I make salad. We sit in the shade; no mosquitoes, a slight breeze. Brier leaps at the cat, who takes none of it. The dog abandons the chase, knocks over my glass of juice and pounces on the ice that clatters across the new grass.

"Judy would love this," I say to Dan.

And tonight, at 11:45, there is no struggle.

———

Brier is running and running. It's her second time out on the agility field, and she doesn't want hoops or ramps. She baulks at the tunnel, doesn't want to enter that dark place. Doesn't care that food awaits her at the end on a small white plate.

She won't come when called, and there is no point chasing her. She can wheel and race faster than any human can run. But she is beautiful to watch. All young fluid muscle, all golden red coat rippling. She is a foal finding her legs. She is a bear cub rolling in the meadow.

"Brier, come!" we call lovingly, then authoritatively, then desperately, having taken our obedience lessons obediently. And she turns to us from the far far corner, knowing she should come. But there's a stronger call than ours. Horses across the road, black, brown and red, toss their heads; manes flying, they whinny. To their challenge, Brier races in wild circles as the whole class watches; she is so stunningly beautiful, so young and alive that even my impatience vanishes. She will come back to us and she knows it. But first she flies over jumps, races up the ramp and down, bounding, whirling, leaping.

She is out of our control, yet in her own, like a rogue race horse, a lone skater on the pond under starlight.

——

I just wish I'd gone up to the lake with Judy, Mum says on one of our phone calls.

She's talking about Judy's last trip to the lake a few weeks before she died. Or maybe a month. No one wrote it down as if they knew the date would be significant. Judy just phoned Mum and said, I'm going up. Do you want to come? And Mum, perhaps because it was hot, or she had something else on the go, or couldn't face her own memories there yet, said, Maybe next time.

Nobody knew, but in my heart I think Judy did. She was going up to say goodbye. I think she kept so much from us, how serious her disease was, how hope was fading, how each hospitalization came closer to being her last.

How could we not have known? And if we did, what could we have done differently? Mum wishes she'd taken that last excursion with her. I could have left my life in BC and moved to Minnesota, but then what? Judy didn't want anyone hovering. She wanted to live her life, go to the hospital when she had to, keep her privacy and her emotional strength. Strength she drew from solitude balanced with laughter and great conversation.

I expect I know what she did those last hours at the lake, alone. She watered the plants on the deck, made coffee, put on her sunglasses, took her book down to the water. Sat on an old slatted chair, read and looked out at the waves on the small lake. Closed her eyes and leaned back, took in the sun. Tried to ignore the small pump attached to her, the relentless rhythm: the push of medication a slight whir and groan. I hope the sounds of wind and waves and the loon's call blocked it out. That her book was good enough, the sun hot enough, and the oak leaves restless in the breeze let her let all that go. That she simply absorbed the power of wind and air and water, the fire of the sun, the solid earth beneath her feet, when she closed her book, then paused every few steps, using the last of her strength to climb back up the slope to the van, to make her trip back home.

———

Don't forget the funny parts, all the good trips, all the laughter, people say when they know I am writing about Judy. But the words for grief are far more powerful, squeezing and releasing like the beat of a strong heart.

Judy and I never forced laughter; it just burbled out of us when we were together, the day's absurdities, our own idiosyncrasies. Together we could laugh at anything, a bad situation with Dad, a very bad motel room, a dinner gone wrong. We'd simply look at each other and lose all control.

My funny Judy stories will come the day when we're side by side again, when our spirits stand together. When she the dead, and me the living, have found our stride together. I expect this. That's the strange thing. I have never expected this before. Not when Dad died, not when my nephew was killed, not when anyone else in my life has expired. I simply didn't expect them to walk next to me again. So how can I tell the funny stories when she's not here to explode into laughter with.

When we told the Winner's Circle Motel story together, people laughed more at us and the tears of laughter streaming down our faces than they did at the actual story. The funny part was us, the absurdity of it all, our complete joy in each other's company.

I would like that balance of light with dark. For every time I've jerked awake at 11:45, the hardwired hour of her death, and shouted her name in my sleep, I would wish for happy hour, when the bottle of wine came out, when the day's stories began. A story Judy would tell of a demanding mother of the bride. Or the time we rescued the pigeon in her chimney, when I made her drag a high ladder into her bathroom so I could cut away ancient wallpaper and remove the grate, to release the trapped and flapping bird. How she, at the bottom of the ladder, cursed all pigeons, rats with wings, she—city girl—called them. And when I finally grabbed the pigeon before it fell lower from its narrow ledge inside the chimney, she was the one who went outside, set up the box with straw and water in a dark place, so it could recover before she set it free, telling it to fly far, far, away.

———

All our lives, through all the obstacles, we mourned and rallied, put on a good face and laughed; our strength supported and drew us all together. Now there is no Judy by my side to mourn her death. I am doing it alone, of course with the love of my faraway family, and the companionship of Dan. But there is no Judy to help me mourn Judy, and I've never really done this alone. I ask myself again if I can ever find the magnificence. Can I ever find such an amazing and graceful path through death?

Her friend Trish Hampl reflected upon Judy's grace and strength: "Move over, Jackie Kennedy," Trish said, and it didn't seem an overstatement, not then, not now.

And odd to say, while I had Judy during those times, she also had me. And right now, there is no me for me to lean on, and that's the navel-gazing truth of the matter. We grieved together, and there is simply no more "we" anymore. The age-old story of losing the people we love, and learning to go on.

There are obvious lessons to be learned: about becoming the driver, learning grace, finding strength, loving and expanding the circle of love. Like patching the broken bricks back together from the mud at the bank of the river.

⎯

July 18 would be her birthday. Sometimes I look at the picture of her on the boat on the Bay of Fundy, and talk to her directly.

But today for the first time I write a letter to her in my journal. It feels odd, almost too deliberate, a note deposited in the dead letter box. But I want so badly to speak with her that I write in my journal what some people would deliver in prayer.

Dear Judy,

You would be sixty-eight tomorrow. From up here in Canada we've ordered flowers, lots of yellows amidst other bright flowers—a bouquet called "Citrus Kissed" for David and Amber, and "New Dreams" for Mum. We ordered them from Johnson's Florists on Grand Avenue. Not sure if they were your florist or not, but sending flowers is a way for Brian, Andy and me to mark your birthday, because we can't visit you at the cemetery.

Today is a lovely day here; some rain finally after a long hot spell, such a surprise that it's raining, or rained and then the sun came out. Dan put up the newest gate to see how it works, and there's more to be done but it's beautiful. He made a jig and wove the hot forged steel, as if it were the delicate lattice of a pie crust.

Funny, with the thunder and fast heavy rains, I thought of the time in Fargo so long ago; it must have been Donna's birthday, as it was tornado season and, while Mum was home baking the birthday cake, you chaperoned a group of us little girls at the movie. The tornado warnings started—sirens that we could hear over the film—and all us little prairie girls knew what to do. Under your calm direction, we headed down to the theatre basement. We were all scared, especially the girls who wanted their parents to come, but you told them their parents had to take shelter at home and that you'd take care of us.

You kept us calm; you always kept calm. I know sometimes you got angry, furious, hurt, wounded; but you somehow gathered it all to you, maybe drew back into yourself, or hashed it out with a trusted friend. But you always had that calm centre with an answer.

The water began rising in the theatre basement. Probably sewers backing up, and so you gathered us and we climbed back up to the first landing.

There was an adult who became hysterical, and you, just a teenager yourself, tied into them in your commanding voice. "Be quiet. Calm down. Act adult, there are children here."

Then out on the street, water ran like a river, and we were excited, relieved, awestruck. Dad drove up in the big old station wagon, like a boat with dirty gushing water to the top of the wheels, and us in our party dresses and black patent leather shoes with little straps. You lifted us over the swift flowing water into the car, where in my memory we squeezed in. No seat belts then, but the safety of you, and Dad, and maybe to seal the story all up in a bundle, our big golden retriever, Dinty. All of us huddled in and began to tell Dad our story.

Judy, this is me, acting adult now and becoming more truly adult each day. Tomorrow you would be sixty-eight to my sixty-one. When you grew so close to dying, before you came home from the hospital, we had those few moments alone when I said, "I wish you had a few more days, Jude," and you looked down as I rubbed your neck, and said, "I do, too," but we knew it was over, and only the final preparations remained to be made.

Shit, I wish you had a few more years.

I can't fight the logic of your death by asking "Why you?" I just can't make any metaphor out of the timing. What is the significance—in a poetic sense—of this order, or what is its meaning? Once when I was writing, and not at the moment of writing, but in a time of writing, I felt a deep and true sense of your own acceptance and wish to get on with it. Writing about you is how I "get on with it." You always understood this. You understood that writing about you, and about us together, would help me. Perhaps you understood it would help us both.

In some ways you are my ghost writer. Oh, that's a sweet way to think of it. Not ghost in the ghastly gruesome sense, but like a spirit, a ghost rider. I have this lovely image of us riding through the badlands, far apart, but sometimes we glimpse each other through the stark landscape, in the mirage of light and sunset. We each know the other is there searching. I like that, as I write in the sunset here, in the gorgeous lights and old windows of our dining room.

Happy birthday, Jude. Wherever you are. In the badlands on a horse you never rode. In the cells of my brain, in the memory of my bones, cooking, tending flowers, on a boat on the ocean, watching whales.

Love you, Jude.

Rita

——

In October 2013, when Andy and I visit St. Paul, our grand-nephew, William, takes his first steps and then walks across the entire living room without falling. In this same week, Andy pounds out a boogie-woogie on the baby grand in the entryway of Mum's place, The Wellington; the fall colours of the maple and oak sway just outside the large windows, and our almost ninety-five-year-old mother beckons me to dance with her.

From the moment we arrived at the airport in Minne-apolis, Andy and I have been in sync and our universe with us. We've flown from opposite sides of the continent, he from Nova Scotia and me from British Columbia, and from the minute our planes set down, things went right. We landed at almost the same moment, each plane arriving early, at gates D5 and D6. Side by side. No searching, no waiting, no frustration. I feel I am back in sync with myself; my very DNA and his are aligned. If we need to be somewhere at a certain time, we are both ready early and leave and arrive on time. There is none of this non-sense where people lag and drag or rush around and keep you waiting and think that's acceptable. No, we are on prairie time, the kind of time we grew up in, where we never leave anyone waiting or stranded, as if any delay could mean frostbite or death from the cold.

This trip is movement; getting on with life. There is no crisis behind this journey. We are simply here to visit our family, especially to be with our amazing mother and our grandnephew who Andy is meeting for the first time.

We could watch him for hours, help feed him, laugh with his laughter. We are childless great-uncle and -auntie, doting upon David and Amber's baby.

They have transformed the second and third floor of Summit Manor, the home David grew up in and Judy lived and died in. On the first floor, David cooks and caters for the big weddings as Judy once did. David and Amber have modernized the kitchen and ripped apart the living space on the second and third floors, redesigned, reinsulated and made a stunning home. A blend of the old and new, the old leaded windows repaired and double paned, their beauty and substance intact.

It took youth and vitality and new ideas to make this happen. Judy couldn't. As I survey the light and spacious third floor, I remember how it had stagnated, had become storage for broken beds, old desks, boxes of unsorted photos, photo boards for all who had died; the photo display for Mike, Judy's husband, who died in 1997, full of gaps from when we removed pictures for stepson Johnny's funeral in 2001, and then we mined Johnny's display for photos of William after the plane crash in 2002, and then Dad in 2003. The third floor, aside from the TV room, had become a mausoleum and in her last years, Judy could never find the strength to transform it. Now it hums with life, a baby, cartoons on the TV and family talking and cooking.

Andy and I take Mum for an autumn drive to visit the family lake place. She is hesitant; she hasn't been there since Judy's death. But she delights at the fall colours and loves the renovations in the cabin. With very little help, she walks down the steep hill to the lake, and we fetch deck chairs, sit by the water on a most beautiful blue Minnesota day. Mum walks the shoreline, picking up shells to wash and save, first inspecting each one for signs of life. We sit contentedly in the sun, watching waves, watching a heron lift and fly. Later we pick tough-skinned apples from the tree Dad planted, and they are sweet and tart all at once.

"I made so many pies with those apples," Mum says. "Dad liked it with a slice of cheddar. Cold, strong cheddar."

How dad-like. Sweet, crisp, hard-skinned apples baked in a homemade crust, topped with cheddar. Not gooey, melted, mild and tasteless cheese, but sharp, hard and cold.

Dad's tree is still producing.

—

I feel on the verge of true happiness; we are simply together and we are happy. Judy is with me, but she moves lightly now, swirls around me sometimes like a wisp of air. We are letting her go somehow. Letting her move, as William does, as Mum does.

She's in the sunrise and sunset, in the dark branches of oak. Through the scattered light of the leaded windows, Judy glimpses her grandson tottering, walking, pushing. Judy's movement now is wind, the sway of tree limbs, the heron rising above the water.

——

Andy plays the piano, to Mum's delight and that of the other residents, when we visit The Wellington. At David and Amber's, he bakes bread, an artisan or peasant recipe, the kind you cook in a pot. This recipe has taken hold all over North America; it's simple and doesn't require the craft of the experienced baker, yet makes delicious fresh bread.

Use any combination of flours, Andy says. He likes some rye and whole wheat. He measures loosely and surely, no flat blade scraping the top of the cup for exactness. It's forgiving, he says. Then the yeast, then salt. He uses so little salt, a sixth of what the recipes call for. It's our family's concession to heart problems—cut down on the salt. And then he adds the luke-warm water, and mixes it but doesn't knead.

The covered dough sits overnight, and by morning is a bubbling mass. He spreads flour on the huge marble table, turns the dough onto it, works it a few times, then cuts it in half. He covers one plate with poppy seeds, one with cornmeal, then sets half the dough on each to rise again.

We are a family of cooks. Everyone has grown up cooking, and I think this is rare in our Presbyterian/Anglo/Prairie culture. That our families, who didn't have the Italian or Greek, Doukhobor or Chinese heritage, still retained and expanded on a kitchen culture. We simply didn't have, or at least we didn't think we had, a specific culture to cook from. But we did. We grew up on Irish stews, porridge every morning, meats and gravies, garden food: tomatoes, onions, corn. Beets and turnips. Northern pike and venison and lots of beef. We grew up with peasant food: good, hearty, nourishing and reliable. Feed lots of people, our family and whoever stopped by; you could always add another slice of bread, extra potatoes, to fill up the plate. Funny now that I think of it, we grew up on a 100-Mile Diet, with the rare exception of canned mandarins and fruit cocktail that tasted like the grey sides of the metal tin.

Mum was head cook, and Dad the second. She turned out the daily rounds of roasts, salads, cakes and cookies, with the occasional foray into the exotic: Chinese stir-fries with MSG, such a craze for a time. Dad cooked lentil stews in the cast iron Dutch oven.

And so we learned, all of us; helped cut and stir, serve, sit down to the table, eat well and clean up later. I can't cook for two people—there is always food for six or seven, always leftovers to reheat or freeze for a busy day.

The recipes I received from Judy, and now from David, are never for six people. Instead they serve the multitudes. Artichoke lasagne for 200; ham dinner for 75; pork loin baked with fresh chutney for 150.

Sometimes as I pass through David and Amber's main floor kitchen where the big catering is done, the kitchen where Judy truly lived between the stove and her office and the round oak table where friends and family gathered, drinking coffee, a glass of wine at night as we watched the news, I see her. Or I remember the thousand times I rubbed her shoulders, the hundreds of times she said, "Red or white?" as she yanked open the heavy metal door of the industrial fridge. The kitchen was always noisy with the big freezer, the big fridge, but a noise you became used to, became alarmed about if there was quiet, oh no, a refrigeration breakdown. Check the fuses, call the fridge guy.

But now as I pass through the big kitchen on this day with no weddings, the lights off and fridge humming steadily, it is a quiet workplace. Family life, food and laughter, have moved upstairs.

On the third floor, as Andy makes the bread, he explains each step, which I write down and photograph, so I can go home and remember and replicate.

Sun streams through the leaded windows and William watches from his baby rocker fastened securely to the middle of the tabletop where Andy works. Or he races around the floor in his wheelie chair. Or, learning to walk now, he explores the pantry, pulls open the bottom drawer, empties it of baking pans, rattles measuring spoons in the air.

Andy's bread is crusty outside, tender in the middle. We slather it with butter; dunk it in the homemade Moroccan soup Amber has prepared. We toast the bread in the morning; transform it into garlic bread at night.

Later, back in our own homes thousands of miles apart at the opposite ends of Canada, we exchange pictures of our home-baked loaves, long distance love, our daily bread.

———

Our sister Donna's daughter Maggie, our niece, gives birth to a baby girl, Georgina. Georgina is named after our maternal grand-mother. Little Georgina is dark-haired and dark-eyed. She will grow into her own self of course, but deep in my heart, I wonder if one day, with her dark hair and complexion, she will look like Judy.

———

For Christmas, Dan and I buy a piano without the indecision we normally go through over a pair of socks.

We unpack the full keyboard Yamaha electric, just the right size for the dining room, which is becoming our music room.

The piano nestles into our lives as surely and securely as did our dog, another decision quickly and well made. These moments of certainty and rightness feel like the round block slipping into the round hole, when so much of life is jamming squares.

The piano sits quietly. Waiting.

There is theory and there is putting hands to keys; I haven't touched a piano since I was ten, when practising meant the strict tutelage of severe Sister Elizabeth, with her upright spine, her habit and her wimple. Though we had no truck with the Catholic Church, piano lessons were with Sister Elizabeth.

We walked around to the back door of the cathedral, which we'd once visited as young Unitarians, wanting to be broad-minded about all religions, and were humbled by the incense, the colour, the pageantry; the poverty of our intellectual simple unadorned Unitarianism so pallid in comparison, even to our young eyes.

And so, Sister Elizabeth met us at the back door, or in the schoolroom, or the church basement, I don't recall, but it was the back of the set, no magnificat, simply an old brown piano and a nun in black and white. Good Boys Do Fine Always, or Every Good Boy Does Fine, I learned, memorizing the black keys and the white, and even then wondering how the girls fared. As if we didn't matter in these artistic endeavours, not enough to get a note in our name, even if there were Gs in every octave.

In my childhood home, the red lesson book leaned lonely at the upright piano in the basement. The rec room was too scary, cold, and anything could leap out from the pantry under the stairs, or scratch at the back screen door, which faced the Red River and where hobos jumped from slow-moving trains and camped by the tracks. They had come to our back door, scratched on the screen in the night, trying to get in, or so my brothers, whose room was downstairs, reported.

I didn't hate the piano, just felt isolated from family life, voices upstairs in the kitchen, supper cooking, doors slamming as brothers and sisters ran in and out; Mum cooked, the dog barked when Dad came home, and I tried to twinkle, twinkle with the little star, alone downstairs, CCGGAAG, how I wonder what you are. No child ever abandoned her piano bench and scrambled upstairs faster on all fours, the bogeyman at my back, when piano practice ended each day.

In our teen years, Andy left the piano behind and took up guitar, and I, dutiful younger and adoring sister, sang alongside him. Later in life, when an accident at the table saw left him without a full middle finger, he gave up guitar and returned to piano. Perhaps inspired by him, and wanting to pick out the harmony lines Dan and I sing in choir, I too return to the keyboard.

In our home the piano is upstairs, where life is, not down in my office that goes cold and empty at night. No, the piano is on the main floor, by the stained glass window, the dining room table, the warmth of the fireplace, the smells of supper cooking.

I am back at Twinkle Twinkle, but aim for greatness: "Stand By Me," with full chords, Gabriel Fauré's Pavane, so familiar as the closer for *Gilmour's Albums* for decades. I try the theme from Mozart's Symphony no. 40, familiar too from CBC, once the source of my musical education. We live where there is no reception for CBC 2 or 3, and where the main CBC no longer plays hours of classical music at night, where there is no eclectic announcer who loves music talking to us and teaching us into the small hours.

And so I reach back in my memory to find those familiar tunes and play them as if at age sixty-one, I might abandon writing and cooking and all other loves to become a concert pianist. I am in love with the piano as I never was as a child.

At each note, my brain and hands struggle, rapidly flipping through Every Good Boy Does Fine, F-A-C-E, Good Boys Do Fine Always, All Cows Eat Grass, straining to find each note in that literary list while attempting to keep a beat, remember the flats and sharps, the notations of *piano* for soft, or *forté* for strong.

Yesterday my mother was diagnosed with Raynaud's Disease, the same disease that began Judy's long struggle. Mum's hand turned blue, her index finger black, for no apparent reason. David rushed her to medical help, thinking it may be a stroke, something gone terribly wrong just a week after her fourth annual visit to the Mayo Clinic where she was declared again as a medical miracle. She breaks down in tears as the nurse warms her cold hand. Is it hereditary, she asks, convinced now of the belief harboured deep in her mother's heart, that she transmitted the disease that killed her daughter.

I sit firmly at the piano bench. Select the difficult chords for "Stand by Me." It is far beyond my level of skill, but somewhere in those clunking chords, movement and life emerges. My hands warm at the keyboard; the plaque clicks and slips from my heart and brain.

I play music for Judy, for my mother, for my father. I play softly for the peace of their souls. Play loudly to the power of their lives.

But mostly, I play for me.

Piano means soft. *Forté* means strong.

CONSOLOTRIX AFFLICTORUM: 2014

Easter is coming and the sun is warm. I've cleaned up the strawberry and flower beds. I stand at every spot I've planted and urge the green shoots of tulips and the yellow tips of daffodils to emerge.

Each day I write agendas or a press release. I consume email like vitamins, practise restorative busyness: important positions, good works. Each day as my meditation I ward off despair with scribbled notes, highlighter pens, the click on, then off, of the printer.

I write nothing about Judy, but she is biding her time, smiling. Her feet are no longer swollen, she is light and airy, she is comfortable again, and she knows and I know that I am simply learning to run again, might even do a jig, the steps my own. I gotta do this, Jude, I tell her, and she smiles and agrees. Knows it is me who tethers her. That it is me who keeps saving her old calls on my voice mail; press "9" to save her messages every forty days lest they erase themselves in a moment when I lose my vigilance.

Judy can wait. She is dead and I expect the dead are practised at waiting. She will simply lie and wait, lie in wait, for me, until I let her go. I don't know what that's like, to let go the string, watch the balloon sail. Will I gasp when her voice no longer greets me on the long-saved messages? When I no longer have any recording of her voice saying, "Oh hi, it's Judy."

My throat swells and aches at the loss of her voice.

It's the third Easter since her death. A time for silence and choirs. A walk by the river with Brier, who is close to three now. She has learned her world. The innocent puppy is gone.

She is a dog of routine. When she senses change or uncertainty, she stops, does not rush toward it, but assesses and tests. She is cautious at first, needs to find her own footing.

She is a beauty in the water. Powerful. Self-assured. She works with the current instead of fighting it.

———

Of course I think about funerals sometimes, since there are so many to attend. As one of my friends about to shuffle off her own mortal coil observed: "They're digging our row."

For our rural burial society, we fill out forms saying what we want or don't want: burial or cremation, what kind of ceremony, all that kind of thing. I immediately reply that I don't want bongo drums or any fake spirituality. Aside from my flippancy, I think deeper and harder and seriously.

I conclude that when I die I want a funeral; a good old-fashioned funeral, not a "celebration of life." I want mourning. I mean real mourning with gnashing of teeth and rending of garments. I am sick of the prettification of death, as if its power should be tamed with saccharine. Please do not displease me with a "celebration of life." I will rise and smite you.

Please do not use euphemisms: don't say I "passed away." Respect the fact that I was a journalist. I did not pass away. I died. Short, simple, declarative.

I did not "pass," as if while you weren't looking, I slipped into a lining of white satin, to save you all the trouble of watching my death throes. I have never experienced the throes of birth and I aim to take my leave with more hard labour than you can bear to watch.

Don't google some "celebration of life" website, with its pastel balloons and little stars and hints for how to plan a lovely brunch in honour of the dearly departed. Little pastel balloons are for a child's birthday party, not for a cleaving of the earth.

You want true celebration? What good funeral doesn't, by its very honesty and integrity, its homage and liberation, inspire great wrenching tears and great wrenching laughter, inevitable when you allow the best speakers—with the well-timed barb, the unexpected lament—to speak, the best poets to recite and singers to sing and the best cooks to cook the best funeral meats. What jazz funeral isn't a celebration, what three-day wake is all solemn? Isn't that the catharsis of a funeral? The rawness, the convulsions and murmurs, the burble of conversation, soft laughter and then the hoot or guffaw from across the room?

Don't plan me a "celebration" all tonied up with pretty colours like a storefront window, all toned down with nice emotions.

Give me a good old-fashioned funeral. Give me black the colour of dirt, give me bonfires and hell and damnation, give me fireworks and clanging bells and explosions.

Throw in some horses with plumes pulling a wheeled hearse with big windows. Put me in a wagon, a pickup truck, the bucket of a tractor. Let everyone see my coffin as I roll by. Let me hear the grunts as my best friends and my family lower me into the grave. Let people cry and hurt and lament to huge sad music. Do all of that: take me out of the hearse and put me under in style, but don't set me up with a celebration.

Did Mozart call his Requiem a Celebration of Life? He would have been tossed from the church, laughed out of Vienna.

Save the celebration of life for those too timid of death.

Give me its ugliness, its pain and grace.

Then bring on the Mozart.

―

It's become an embarrassing reality. My attention span is fractured and I can't cope with big issues. Even now, several years since my sister's death, my mind is so fragmented that I would rather read recipe books than a good novel.

So, I cook: food is tangible and beautiful, its challenges a puzzle with an answer. I stand in my pantry and wonder how I will combine a jar of peaches with a pork roast from the freezer. Would it work to cook lamb with plums and leeks?

I never want to be without salsa, six jars in the pantry. Coffee; when we're below five pounds, I check for the sales.

Olive oil and sun-dried tomatoes from Ferraro's, the Italian store in Trail. The freezer is full of chicken and lamb, tortillas and hamburger. Oh just think of the wonderful things I could make on a moment's notice, if, say, the hillside slid down—a muddy torrent—and everyone were cut off, the phones, the power, the highway, as has happened. How then I, and an equally compulsive neighbour, could feed hundreds for days, our larders full and welcoming.

This is my religion, the generosity, the grace and spirit of food. In the kitchen, I concentrate and create. I banish all annoyances, all daily worries and pettiness. The kitchen must be clean, my thoughts clear. The kitchen is my meditation zone, my journal, my church, my dance floor.

—

In our backyard, Brier dances through the six weave poles stuck into grass and dirt. The turf is soft on her feet as she weaves among the familiar homemade poles, so unlike our agility trainer's regulation equipment. The trainer's poles have metal bases connecting them; the metal feels strange on Brier's feet, and she is cautious.

In our trainer's field, Brier is distracted by the horses across the road; she has to walk around the weave poles to see if they're trustworthy. When I give her the command to "Weave," she dopes through them as if they're simply an obstacle on her way to something she prefers: the ramp, or staring at the horses. We try again, and again she acts as if she's never done it.

I, too, am being cautious, then I throw it to the wind and yell, "GO, GO, GO!" as I do at home, and she snaps to, races through the poles, not missing one. The change in her behaviour is so striking that we—the teacher, other students, and me—are dumbfounded.

Okay, says the instructor, Linda, slowly. She speaks to me kindly, as if something has been achieved here that no one quite understands. How did this goofy, sometimes reluctant, overcautious or even rebellious dog manage such beautiful work?

Do you know if she usually goes through with two feet leading, or if she leads with one? No, I say, I just know she goes through.

Linda asks us to do it again, only this time, that I not be quite so excited, not to bark the GO, GO, GO! so enthusiastically. Brier is beautiful. She responds to my tone like a racehorse to the hands of a good jockey. Weave, I say: go, go, go. Instead of bouncing through the poles like a rocking horse, she shifts into a beautiful stride. She leads with her inside foot, dances through the poles, leans and twists with every sinew of her strong young body. She is gold and red threading the poles, and everyone watches, wondering what just happened. Brier is ecstatic, and then rushes to the ramp to run up and down. They're not supposed to go to the next obstacle without being given direction, but as I call to stop her, Linda calls out, "Let her!" It's a reward, and given that freedom, she races over the ramp with me right beside her, then she levitates over jumps and through the tunnel, its darkness she once feared now a race to the light.

I am so proud of her. So proud of me. She came into my life when grief sat heavy. She made me laugh. She mirrored my caution at change; she walked around it with me, worked through fears and, one step at a time, over and over every day, we are finding our way through.

The instructor says to increase the poles to eight, so she doesn't pattern too much on coming out of the weave after six. At home I go out by the garden shed, find old pieces of rebar and lengths of discarded water pipe and make more weave poles. Brier watches, wary. I have treats, and a very short leash. We'll do this slowly, again one step at a time. No rushing. We don't want mistakes or discouragement. She wants to leave after the sixth pole, as she has done previously to such triumph. "All the way," I coach gently, "All the way."

——

Judy has stepped aside. Physically and metaphorically.

And now I am changing.

Judy never tried to stop me so she could stay in charge. But she was my chairwoman, my president, and I accepted her final say, her fully and well-thought-out decision. We never needed a vote. It was always by consensus, with Judy drawing our conclusion together like pulling the string at the top of a bag. There. Done. Decided. We're in good shape. Let's do it.

But there is no denying that she has stepped aside now, and there is a vacuum to fill. There is no one else I will allow to fill her shoes.

Except for one term as president of our provincial writers' federation, I've rarely been in charge. I've usually been a vice-president, the one who calls the president and says, what if we did this, or we have to remember that.

But I am changing.

An organization I had helped found two decades ago when I was forty-three—our seniors' housing society—was in trouble, with board after board resigning. A friend implored people to attend a special meeting to find out what was going on.

So at age sixty-three, as I walked into the seniors' lodge, which I had helped to build, the same place I take yoga under the big skylight, people sat alone and rigid, or stood in small clusters, speaking only to a few. There was no food, no laughter, no mingling. No hospitality.

Remaining board members, angry, deflated, divided, quit. After the resignations and a complete collapse of leadership, there was a surprising calm in the room. I looked around me. I was surrounded by people I love, wise political people I've worked with for decades, people who have been scarred and who have recovered, who understand exactly what is needed in such a moment. To my surprise, a tenant nominated me to stand for a completely new board, a clean slate. I looked to the rows behind me, to people beside me. We looked into each other's eyes and with no words, knew what to do. With a simple exchange of glances, a motion proposed, a knowledge of rules and constitutions and agendas, without a single objection, without ever planning this, we became the new board.

That evening, in our small but confident group, I was happy. I felt stability had returned, that we were wise and ready, and that I would head this board if asked. And so I became president.

I like it. I like to plan and prepare, to think far ahead, to set goals. All my years of negotiating, listening, congregating the right people for the right purpose, serve me well.

I am not trying to be Judy. I am being fully me. I don't have Judy to consult with, but her example taught me well. As did our mother's. An ability to see far ahead, a brain for details, a nose for smelling out nonsense and meanness and stopping it firmly but kindly. I don't aim to please everyone, but I don't have any wish or need to be unkind.

I remember when people my age were new to this community. We were the twenty-year-olds looking to the fifty-year-olds as our anchor, to those who had a life of experience and who would reassure us. Now I am sixty-three, and it is the ninety-year-olds who nod their heads in affirmation of our work. When they are gone, we'll be the sages. Already the young people ask about history, about how we started our rural institutions and movements.

People say you can't really be an adult until your parents die. I have never believed this, think it's the same kind of pontificating tripe that claims you have to reject or hate your parents and break from them. I know many people—particularly women—who loved their parents and built their own fulfilling lives without the necessity of rejecting them. Several of my best and most calm friends have loved their parents throughout their life, and their parents' deaths gave way to an orderly transition.

But it is also true that having someone to help you make decisions is such a blessing that you don't truly understand their strength until it's missing. Their ability to round things out, to say a kind word when someone is hurting. To phrase it just so, so the point is made but the person saves face, comes out from the dark place and rejoins the circle.

I will find that ability now, in the midst of people I love and trust.

I am maturing.

— — —

I send my family a short video of Brier racing through the weave poles. "Brier weaving," says the subject line. Andy writes back: "Wow, weaving. I'm going to show Shep—he can't even knit."

Andy asks the distance between the poles used in this agility routine. I race out with my camera, set up the bright orange measuring tape between poles. Call Brier. She stares down at the tape, confused. Chutney, the cat, always curious and imperious, saunters over, weaves in front of Brier, arching her back and tail against the poles. Snap, snap goes the camera. In the fourth shot, Brier looks down at the tape as if she finally comprehends.

"Brier says the interval is two feet," I write beneath the photo.

Brian, the cat brother, gives Chutney the credit. Then claims his cat can crochet.

I love this back and forth.

I can't help but say it: it's the warp and woof of our family weave.

———

David and Amber's daughter, Avery, is born in May. More baby pictures, of William and Avery, of Mum holding Avery, of Avery meeting Buchanan, their big golden retriever. Kids and their great nana and the family dog. What could be better?

———

Judy would be sixty-nine today, says my mother, who is ninety-five. We're on the phone, and Mum is happy about the bouquet of yellow sunflowers we've sent. Yellow is the colour that Judy and Mum both liked.

Tell me about Judy's birth, I say.

There are some images you never forget, my mother answers. It was my first birth, and it took a long time.

What hospital? St. Boniface?

I can't remember now, she says. Sometimes I get mixed up between Winnipeg and St. Paul.

There was Fargo, too. You had five kids in three different places.

Yes, but Judy was Winnipeg. And the image I'll never forget is when the nurse took her away from me. Judy wasn't eating well, and they had to take her down the hall. I remember she was such a small bundle, and the nurse put her over her shoulder and I could see her face. I started crying then because I didn't want them to take my baby away from me.

Always in these phone calls, we move away from and back to Judy. The well of sadness is too deep and we can never dive to the bottom.

Mum talks about a new kind of cat food her eighteen-year-old cat loves. She talks about her exercise classes; how she attends three a day sometimes.

What kind of classes? I ask, while still thinking about that image of Judy at birth.

Well, the regular kind, where you move your arms and legs. Then a kind where it's more like dance movements.

Dancercise.

Yes, that's it. And then yoga in a chair. So you get all your parts going if you do all three. I'm down to 116 pounds.

Pretty soon your age and weight will be the same, I say. How are your new glasses?

The line across the middle is a nuisance, but I'm adjusting.

In the dark room as Judy lay dying, Mum sometimes moaned with grief and exhaustion. She crawled up on Judy's big bed with her, and they slept together. It kills me. It kills me still. Judy's breathing so laboured, both of them so tired, as if the labour were reversing, and my mother knows that once again she will see her child being taken down the hall.

I'll never stop missing her, she says.

I'm not afraid of dying, says Mum. Really. But while I'm living I just want to live. I'm very careful about what I eat. I don't eat desserts and I don't take a drink. Except for Guinness on special occasions. Or wine when you're here. And I don't eat after supper. Oh, I could complain about not hearing so well, but with a lot of people you don't want to hear what they have to say anyway, so it works out.

I wish for my mother's lightness, her "grit your teeth and get on with it" Irish pluck. But my personality combines my parents': her laughter and smart mischievous eyes and my father's dark Scottish brooding. I plunge sometimes, like him, and I sit staring, wonder what's down there at the bottom. My mother is my mermaid, calling me back to the light.

How must it have been for her that Judy, the likeness of Dad, could no longer come to the surface?

I'm glad the image my mother will never forget is Judy's birth. For me it is her death. Yes, there are the days and weeks, years of fun we had together, but Judy and I dealt with so much death together. It is not obsession, or at least I hope it isn't. It's the core of deep deep trust we built upon, knowing exactly when in grief it's the very best to erupt into laughter, and laugh so hard you weep again.

Her courage, when her stepson's strong body wouldn't give up, though the brain tumour had shut everything else down, and the exhausted family was called again and again to his bedside, and she said honestly: "Johnny needs to die now."

How after Dad's death, the young woman at the funeral home wanted to make sure we knew cremation wasn't reversible, and we laughed so hard we wept.

I want her laughter to buoy me when I am confused and incompetent, low and tired. When she would tease me, bring me back, with singular advice: "You can do it." Or, "Rita, take a nap." Or, "How about supper out?" or "Ready for wine?"

I know other women who have lost their big sisters, the light of their lives. It's not as if we are floundering incompetents who only kept afloat in their wake. We have our own interests, skills, communities of friends. But there is that difficult transition, when you can't step into their shoes, never could in the family dynamic, and you can't simply transfer your dependency. You just have to grow up more, and it doesn't matter if you are sixteen or sixty, you have to, and do, transform. There is no longer that leadership to look to; the "decider" is gone. And for only so long can you call on her shared wisdoms, only so long can you say, "What would Judy say, think, do?" It simply has to be, "What am I going to say, think, do?"

——

It's Labour Day weekend, 2014, and hot hot hot. Today is Brier's first agility competition, at Pass Creek Park near Castlegar. Dan and I help unload equipment: huge ramps, barrels of stakes, rolls of orange fencing, heavy teeter-totters and poles for fences, bulky tunnels, and more poles for the weave. Now and then we look up from our tasks to see the mountains and think how lucky we are to be outside, with tents and wind and sun rather than inside a crowded and sterile arena.

Brier wants to run all over to smell everything; to dive shoulder first into deer shit, or savour the deep and lasting aroma of a small piece of hot dog dropped by a child at the last event. Her nose is in overdrive, her ears on alert. But in this environment with so many dogs, she has to be kept on a leash, and I snap at her: "Brier, don't pull!"

This Friday night of the agility trial is a "fun night," so the dogs can get a feel for the ring and the equipment, and do some practice runs before the competition starts tomorrow. I tell myself I don't care about winning, but I harbour a sweet private scenario: that Brier will awe the judges and spectators. That her golden coat, her fluid lope that covers the ground so unpretentiously, the way she gathers herself and never knocks down the bar on a jump—will cause a hush around the ring. Dogs will cease barking. Birds will cease chirping. All eyes will be on Brier and breaths will be held until the final roar of hurrah. Brier and I, modestly, will accept their ovation.

In an agility competition, the handlers first walk the course without their dogs. Course map in hand, we figure out how to approach and complete each numbered obstacle in the prescribed order: weave poles, tunnels, ramp, teeter-totter, A-frame, bench and jumps. The dogs have no chance to practise the actual route of the course, which changes for every category in the trial. When it's their turn to compete, they are completely dependent upon signals and commands from their handlers. Handlers can't touch the dogs; the dogs are not wearing collars and no treats or toys are allowed in the ring. It's all about intelligence, love and training.

On this "fun night," Dan hides with his camera far from where Brier could notice him. Don't stress, say the organizers, no one is really watching your dog, they're thinking about their own. No one believes this because we all clap and moan or laugh at every dog's attempt, and we know the experienced competitors—supportive as they may be—are eyeing the new entries.

When our turn comes, instead of jumping over it, Brier runs past the first hurdle. I coax her back to the start line, and try again. She clears it beautifully and on to the next. And the next. Then she refuses the ramp. She has never refused the ramp. She loves the ramp. We try again, and she slinks over it as if I'm about to clean her ears and clip her toenails. We get past the ramp and she jumps some more, then races through a tunnel from the wrong direction. No matter. It's a "fun night." We simply need to finish and smile. Like competitive skaters after a fall, their hips and legs covered in ice, a rictus grin pasted on their chops. Brier jumps well, then senses something, someone, stops abruptly and runs to the fence, faces Dan where he films us from the steps of a building far away. I give up the course, coax her to the exit and out.

The owner of another golden retriever enters the ring after us. They do everything perfectly. Speedily. Efficiently.

"Oh Brier," I say, "you tried, didn't you? You're a good girl." We go far away from the ring and the perfect dogs to play Frisbee. She catches it every time.

I tell Dan to erase the video.

The next time in the ring, Brier is better, not so distracted. She flies over jumps, we ignore the ramp, she is happy happy and doing well, until she squats to pee at the weave poles. Instant elimination, an apt word. It happens to everyone, say the kind people in the ring crew as they mark the spot and run over with the bottle of vinegar as we make our exit.

The other golden retriever again does perfectly.

On her third try, Brier improves again until she sees someone outside the ring playing ball with their dog. "Sorry," says the ball bouncer. "It's called ring proofing," says another. "Your dog has to stay focused in the ring no matter what's going on outside."

I am losing my awoof and happy demeanour.

The owner of the perfect golden retriever approaches to offer consolation and advice. "My dog used to be like yours," she offers kindly, but I scent a not so subtle implication that my dog is stupid, undisciplined, slow, incapable of understanding the basics, and handled poorly. "I can tell you how to fix her," she continues.

"She doesn't need fixing, you stupid cow," I want to shout, in a most unfeminist and competitive manner. "She's perfect how she is! She's young, she's beautiful, and your fucking dog will have arthritis and fleas when Brier comes into her own."

"Thank you, we're fine," is what I actually splutter and huff off in a way that now makes me cringe, since I've since met this woman again and truly she is kind. But in that moment, I didn't want her advice or that of anyone but my own people. I take Brier for a swim. Brier's a country dog. She's rarely on a leash; she lives to run and swim, wrestle with her friends, chase a ball and annoy the cat. She loves agility training, but this isn't training. She's distracted and distressed. This isn't "fun."

The next day is Saturday, the first day of the actual competition, and our own agility teacher will be present. I wrote to her late Friday night, saying how discouraged I am. She tells me it's normal, that she'll be there the next day, and all Brier's dog friends from the class will be, too. Things will be better and Brier will feel more secure. And we'll figure out some ways to handle it all.

That next day, Brier is calmer. So am I. Help is here. People she knows. People I know. Dogs she knows. My classmates pet her, say, "Hi, Brier," and she squirms with delight. She is such a golden retriever. Through the morning, I can see her gathering. I can feel it. She watches her dog pals in the ring sometimes, though I don't let her watch too much. She takes in how they do it and listens to the cheers. Our agility teacher walks us to the waiting area outside the ring, gives me a special treat to give Brier so she will focus on me before we enter.

It works. The only mistake is mine, not hers. Probably all the mistakes have been mine all along. Because she watches closely, she is aware of the turn of my shoulder, of my eyes going to the next hurdle before she has entered the one we're on. It has been my confusion that confuses her, my insecurity that makes her hesitate. This time, we are calm, don't try for speed, just opt for grace and joy. She is so pleased, so happy. She levitates over jumps, races for the ramp, corrects mid-air if I correct a signal. We're a team. We may not be the fastest team, or the most accomplished, but this time we leave the ring trotting, heads up.

There is one more competition for us. There are seventeen obstacles. The heat is withering, the dogs and handlers exhausted. And as they flag, Brier comes into her own. All her country muscles, all her races through the forest, all her long days of play and swimming, all her training on our funky backyard agility run, all her conditioning, it all comes together. She pays attention. She does not miss a single obstacle until I make a slight mistake at number 14, but we regroup and she ends the run with a difficult turn in the proper direction, and I holler out, "Yay Brier!" And the crowd laughs and claps.

Our teacher grabs me in a magnificent hug. The owner of the other golden retriever does not appear to offer advice.

What we do next is an anticlimax, but I want to do it. Because things are running ahead of time, they allow a rerun, not for points, but just for the training. Brier nails every single obstacle; she's confident; she's flying, she's beautiful, she's fluid; she's molten gold.

It's quiet, I notice. Dogs have ceased their barking, birds their chatter.

"Brier," I say, my face to hers, "We did it." And we, modestly, because really no one is watching anymore, return to our tent.

———

Today, September 5, is the third anniversary of Judy's death. I can't believe I didn't remember until Brian wrote an early morning email from Winnipeg.

I rarely jerk awake now at 11:45 p.m. The days have become full of work and play and purpose, exhaustion, laughter and fulfillment. I am refilling my cup, and my sister's laughter—her Judyness—is returning to flush out the pain of her final hours.

Today, for example, I followed through on a notice from the phone company that all old voicemails would be erased unless I took steps to save them permanently. I talked long distance to a young woman who, understanding my lack of technological skills, transferred all the voice mails to my computer. I shared them with my family, who through power failures or mistakes, have lost their own record of Judy's voice.

It is comforting even in its irony to hear her assurances: "Well, the good news is that I'm getting better, and that's what we want." That was just a few months before she died. In another message, she tells me about an annoying phone call she received and asks me to be her surrogate.

"I can't drink anymore because of the medication, but could you drink about eight glasses of wine for me?"

Last night Dan and I attended a concert in a beautiful straw-bale house, its huge wooden beams, gorgeous glass vases, metalwork and sculptures all original work by the owners and their friends. The music is classical piano and violin. I see a friend from our choir, David, there for the first time without his wife, Susan. Susan died from cancer and we have just buried her in our local cemetery. Susan's sister Marjorie sits next to David, and as the music begins, he sobs so violently that his entire body convulses. I move to him, take the wine that threatens to fly from his glass, hand it to a friend, sit next to him, buffer him on his left side as Marjorie does on his right. He settles and takes my hand a moment, and can once again hold his glass of wine.

When the music ends he tells me it's by Fritz Kreisler, a piece he and Susan loved. He didn't know it would be performed. They had planned to attend this concert together, until her final seizure came after months of treatment for bone cancer.

I've reached the place with Judy's death that I can recognize what a person needs and what they don't need when they are grieving. This is his grief alone, and his family's. As a friend, I can offer small help at such moments, and acknowledge but not try to take over or match his grief. In that moment I could have told him I know what he's going through, that this day is the third anniversary of Judy's death, but part of wisdom is simply this: at this moment, it is his moment. Stay quiet. Share a glass of wine. There will be another time for stories.

There's Something in a Name: 2015

Last night I dreamt of Judy. The first casual kind of dream I can recall; not fraught with meaning as was the dream of our horses running side by side through the desert. The details of this one, the van she drove, the way we nosed our cars together, are the direct influence of a TV show and a movie I've watched in the last few days, staying warm in bed with a sore throat and cold. A dream influenced by codeine.

This is her first appearance in a year.

We arrive at a mall parking lot simultaneously, smile at each other as we each slip into the entry lane, then she swings one way and I the other, come together and park nose to nose. I'm in a beat-up Toyota. She's in a Westfalia, one I just saw on a TV show about touring in Scotland.

We get out of our cars. Hug. Hi Jude. Hi Rit. There's really not much to say. How glad we are to see each other again is so obvious we don't have to say it aloud. I don't even know who said what, it was so mutual.

"Ready?"

"Yep."

"Where should we go?"

And that's it.

We open the doors to her van, and the dream ends.

I so rarely have room now for dreams, for quiet or boredom that breeds images. Being this sick means things stop. Meetings, rehearsals. No energy for doing taxes or other busy important things. So I shut down, go inside myself, somewhere I haven't been for a long time.

I read a book of fiction about a dog rescue sanctuary on a mountainside, and the troubled young woman who learns her own quiet and strength. Reread a book about dog agility training. Read about a man trying to find his child.

Drink tea. Listen. Open.

Easter is coming, the fourth since her death. Five will be some kind of special marker. We'll say the things you would expect. *Five years, can you believe it? It seems like yesterday.*

But even at four years, let alone five, it *doesn't* feel like yesterday. The intervening years have taken some toll. I am an older person, less ready for adventure; I often get sick before I have to travel.

So I am glad Judy came to me in that dream—just that sense that we'd take off on an adventure. Come on, let's go. Ready?

That's what I say to my dog when it's time for a bike ride on the rail trail, when we're off to do agility, when she has a ball in her mouth and is so eager. With Judy, I was like that eager puppy, and was always ready to do something with her. No question.

Nobody in my life now says: Ready?

Dan and I march along each day, him practising clarinet, or out in the shop pounding metal. We cook together, read books in quiet companionship. Go out to support good causes, sing together in choir, and have many friends. We spend endless hours at the computer, with his work for the burial society, or Riverwatch, and now the board of our community hall. I spend endless hours with our seniors' housing project, chairing meetings, moving things forward. Dan talks about trips abroad, but I cling to routine, a drowning sailor on a two-by-four.

My head hurts and no drug will help. My throat aches and the sky outside is dull, heavy, waiting. My office is stale with old piles of paper, projects in boxes on the chesterfield and the ironing board. Taxes spread out for sorting into the categories and costs of office space and heating bills, the receipts for whiteout and printer cartridges awaiting their proper order.

These doldrums are so unusual—even in my deepest grief, I rarely grew logy. I know these dead days are necessary; in another day or two I will sprint back into action, appalled at this laziness, this inability to get a grip. I'll do the taxes in a frenzy, all set out with totals highlighted in yellow ink, yellow post-it notes adhering to any anomaly.

But for now I am in dreamland, a murky purgatory of coughing spasms that leave me breathless; I sit up and read late into the night, high on a mountain rescuing dogs or searching for a lost child.

That's when Judy comes to me, as if I am the lost one who needs rescue.

Ready?

I don't believe in God, I don't believe in heaven or hell. But still... still... I've heard people who say—upon some life and death crisis on the operating table—that someone they loved beckoned down the tunnel.

If Judy's driving a Westfalia down that tunnel, leans out her window and asks, Ready? I'll be tearing open the door.

Or so I would like to think.

The honest-to-god truth now?

As I grow more into myself?

I don't know anymore if I would race down that tunnel.

—

I got some lab results that unsettled me. High cardiovascular inflammation: not good, said both the doctor and the pharmacist. I have to take it seriously, have to change my diet, get more exercise, manage stress more effectively, take supplements. It's a first test and who knows, it could be the result of months of bronchial infections. But there's no denying our family has a history of heart problems, and Judy's led to her death. In this instance, I obviously do not want to follow in her footsteps. I can't quite get a grip on these health issues—the thyroid problems, and now the heart stuff. I've always been the strong-as-a-horse sister, the traveller, the chainsaw wielder, the table lifter and chair stacker. It's time to make some lists. Make them on big coloured construction paper and pin them to the refrigerator: "More Fish, Fewer Chips," "Eat Flax!" and other annoying and unappetizing reminders.

Perhaps the next lab test will be fine, the first one an anomaly. But I have to take stock, be still with this awhile.

——

My lists have kept me from drifting, but now I am listless.

Life seems to be going awry, or not according to plan, if I had a plan.

I'm sixty-three, semi-retired, and have been offered a job gutting chickens. It's come to this, I think. Chicken gutter. Geek. A circus act kind of person who bites the heads off chickens.

To make it worse, there's a clip on CBC that night from a kitschy movie: "At least I'm not working at the abattoir!" declares the character.

Oh my god, I say to the bathroom mirror as I brush my teeth, I'm going to work at the abattoir.

I'm a rural writer scrabbling for cash. I like the people who own the farm where the chickens are processed. I don't have other big money jobs in the offing. I accept.

I have no illusions about what the job entails. Or entrails, more accurately. As a young hippie decades ago, I butchered many chickens; butchered bears as well. I am not squeamish and know that the meat we eat was once prowling the hillsides or pecking around the backyard clucking and luffing its gorgeous feathers. Or, as a flock, ripping a live mouse apart in a blood frenzy. I don't romanticize chickens, though I have loved their silly sweet fearless companionship at other times in my life.

The chickens we will kill are raised locally and most are organic, and so I work to convince myself of why I should take this job: that I'm not just sucking chicken guts in my sixties, when many around me have retired, but rather, I am contributing to the means of production; I am now not just growing my own meagre broccoli plants, but am about to be initiated as a full-fledged worker in the local agricultural renaissance.

And so I don my layers, from blue jeans to gumboots to kerchief, and with my neighbour, Mireille, rejoin the proletariat, sisters on the production line, Rosie the Riveters, lunch buckets in hand. We wind down the narrow roads to Tulaberry Farm in Passmore, site of Passmore Pluckers, the poultry dispatch unit. The drive through the cedar forest past small farmsteads is lovely in the cool of the summer morning; we know that after a long day slaughtering, we'll drive home again through its shade and quiet.

As the killing begins outside the processing trailer, at first I avert my eyes from the dying birds and stare at the trailer steps. But later, I want to witness, more than anything. I ask to watch, so I am not hiding and waiting for the dead and somewhat sanitized bird to come through on its shackle. I don't want to be one of those production workers who won't look at the start of the line. And, I've always been just plain curious.

The killing is humane. The bird is placed, alive, head-first into a cone, and then the back side of an electric knife is rubbed against its neck and discharges a current that temporarily scrambles its brain. The knife is turned round and the bird's throat is cut. It is so fast: there is no screaming, no fear. The circle of cones moves round, the next bird dies and the sound of daily farm life goes on.

Inside the abattoir we eviscerate, scoop out the lungs, use a vacuum aspirator to suck up the remaining innards—kidneys and such—fine pluck it, wash and plunge the bird into ice water. From live in the crate to cooling in the ice bath takes about fifteen minutes.

I've worked in jobs like this before, but processing vegetables, not animals. In southern Alberta, to pay tuition, I worked on the processing line of Macdonald's Consolidated, which provided frozen corn and carrots for Safeway. We stood on metal ramps high off the floor, as the corncobs or carrots came through. There was a tedious rhythm to the work: the whole line of women doing the same job, with jokes and laughter rising above the noise. It's the rhythm in vegetable processing plants on the prairies, in fish processing plants on the coast, and now here in this abattoir in the mountains.

At lunch we eat outside under a large canopy. Some workers remove their hairnets, but others of us don't bother, and perhaps looking ridiculous in our red, green or white, we are all glad to be off our feet. Some of us see each other only at work, but in our small valley, most everyone knows everyone, or is only a few steps removed. We talk about car accidents and benefit fundraisers, how other farmers are doing, who has which kind of dog, how long will the teachers be on strike, how's the bakery doing, who had eye surgery.

In the fall we will process turkeys, the magnificent birds so beautiful and sweet. The man who kills them handles them gently. They go quietly, and there is a sadness at the end of the day. The morning in the farmyard at first so full of their chortles and calls, and later, silent.

———

One of the abattoir owners is named Judi. There is a generation of Judys in their sixties or seventies. They surround me. As if they are a light blanket, or the door that opens to the sun and a light wind that ruffles my hair.

In my life, in my neighbourhood, there is a Judith, a Judi and two Judys.

Judith, my old friend who I interview for a story, Judy in choir, Judi who I work for, Judy skiing on the rail trail.

I feel a lightness in my voice now when I call out, "Hi Jude!" Or, "See you soon!" I don't pretend I am saying *her* name, as if my friends are substitutes. But to be able to say *Judy* in everyday conversation comforts me, gives me a secret moment of calling out to her in a casual way. Her name is no longer the name I see only in an obituary, or hear on the preserved-in-amber answering machine message; her name is part of everyday commerce.

It's funny, isn't it, how when you're not done with someone, you keep running into them? Like when you're in a fight with someone in the community and the fight isn't truly over, even if it's officially over. But it's there, every day; you see that person driving by when you're walking across the bridge, they're buying the paper as you pay for gas; as if you haven't finished rubbing each other the wrong way.

So maybe it's the same when you haven't let go of someone you love, either. Judys are everywhere. These women with the same name are symbols of unfinished wonderful business; they buoy me by being near, though they may or may not be aware of the new sweetness of their names. How lovely that they allow me to say her name again in so many ways.

And I find it interesting how the women with the name Judith, Judy—women of a certain generation—somehow *are* alike.

The Judys and Judiths and Judes are usually a few years older than me. They are smart, practical, storytellers, shrewd, successful laughing women with large circles of friends. I consider every Judy I know, here and afar, and I don't know any who are whiners or losers, selfish or friendless. Perhaps it's because the name was so popular at the end of the Second World War. How many post-war babies named Judy were the first in the family birth order; how many took care of their younger sisters and brothers? How many Judiths became the responsible ones, decision makers, trusted?

The Judys I know are all women I can count on. They would take me in their arms in a minute, or perhaps chide me, or tease out the knot in my heart. When I am too tired, trying too hard, they would tell me to take a nap, or stop, have a glass of wine.

I call out to the Judys in my life. I don't feel ridiculous that in so doing, I also call out to my sister. Because there really is something in a name.

Each night I see a picture of Judy as I open the window just above her photograph. She's on the boat on the Bay of Fundy. Dark hair, dark glasses, looking to the ocean. Her seventieth birthday's coming up.

Hi, Jude, I say to her photo. It's me. Rita.

Easter: 2016

Brier and I head out on our traditional walk by the river, to the same spot we visited when she was young. Since we came here that first time back in 2012, someone has made a small memorial garden, planted bright yellow, purple and white crocuses, a splash of colour near the bench above the water.

We take this walk together every Easter, and because it has become routine I don't expect miracles or epiphanies. They don't come when I am looking for them. I have no profound thoughts—just throw Brier's ball for her as we walk along the rail trail.

I hide behind trees to see how long it takes before she tears back to me, and then try something I've never done; I lie face down on the trail. Will she be my heroine? Will she think I'm injured, even dead? Will she lick my face or run for help?

I peek through my fingers as she barrels toward my prone form and then, out of my vision, pauses. I feel the thud of the ball as she lobs it into the middle of my back.

I laugh so hard that there is absolutely no doubt, for her or for me, that I am alive.

Ready?

Epilogue: 2017

Easter Sunday, April 16

Mum is ninety-eight. Her brother, Hec, who died many years ago, has just come to visit. She said it was so good to see him striding down the hall like that.

Hillary Clinton was with her the night of the election defeat.

"With you in your heart?" I ask.

"No, she was here. And she was so upset."

"Jackie Kennedy came to visit," she adds. "And Justin Trudeau calls every so often. He's a fine young man… I always liked his father."

These people arriving in the night are not strangers. They're with our family in the photos that sit on her mantle. We've met many of them in our political life in Manitoba and Minnesota: the Trudeaus, both generations; Stanley Knowles and Tommy Douglas; the Kennedys and Clintons.

Who am I to say their latest visits aren't real? They're real to her. I keep learning from my mother. Maybe she'll teach us what's next. What's after. I hope Judy visits and tells Mum she's drinking wine with friends or down by the lake, reading a book.

⎯

I fly to Minnesota on Easter Sunday. At the Shalom Home, where Mum lives her last days, she lifts a Guinness and raises her fist, a kind of salute to make us smile as she takes a small sip and poses. *Click* go our cameras.

The next day she only finds her way to the surface to say hello. Often, she calls out for her mother.

The last day, a musician settles her harp at Mum's bedside and plays "Danny Boy" and "When Irish Eyes are Smiling." Mum dies within the hour. With the help of the undertaker, four generations of our family and a neighbourhood friend prepare her and wrap her body. We wheel Mum down the hall, enveloped in her comforter, her hair a halo around her face, the cane Dad made lying along her side. It is a glorious, laughing, crying send-off.

Irish music playing, she takes her leave in grand style, and in her leave taking, restores the natural order.

Acknowledgements

Thank you.

First to my sister, Judy McLaughlin, and my mother, Erin Moir, for being storytellers who trusted me to tell theirs.

To my family, living and late, far and wide in our big tent, the Moirs, Brian, Andy, and Donna, and our late father David Ross; to my sister-in-law Chris Callaghan; and to the McLaughlins, David and Amber and extended clan, and friends in Manitoba, Nova Scotia, Minnesota and British Columbia.

To Amber McLaughlin for the watercolour—based on a family photo—that graces the cover of this book.

To my Brilliant and Insightful writing group in Nelson, BC: Anne DeGrace, Sarah Louise Butler, Verna Relkoff, Jane Byers, Vangie Bergum, Kristene Perron, Donna Macdonald and Jennifer Craig.

To trusted readers for their critiques: Bonnie Evans, Nancy Flight, Barbara Pulling, Trish Hampl, Ruth Porter and Sabbian Clover.

For their help and support along the way: Lynne Van Luven, Caroline Woodward and Diane Morriss.

To poets Trish Hampl and LeAnn Littlewolf for permission to quote their work. And to the families named in this work, who graciously gave me their permission.

For support during early drafts, the Slocan Valley Arts Council and Columbia Kootenay Cultural Alliance.

To Vici Johnstone, Sarah Corsie, Patricia Wolfe and Malaika Aleba at Caitlin Press for supporting this work and that of many rural women.

To trainer Linda Murray and all the friends, furry and otherwise, who make dog agility so much fun.

To my partner, Dan Armstrong, for his love and endurance and the joyful noise ringing from his shop, and for our housemates, Brier and Chutney.

ABOUT THE AUTHOR

PHOTO DAN ARMSTRONG

Rita Moir lives in the Slocan Valley of BC, where she worked for decades as a freelance journalist for the *Globe and Mail*, CBC Radio and regional publications. CBC also produced and broadcast several of her plays for a national audience. She is the award-winning author of the short story *Leave Taking*, about preparing a body for burial (event non-fiction winner, Norton Reader, Best Canadians Essays); *Survival Gear* (Polestar, 1994), shortlisted for the Edna Staebler Award for Creative Non-Fiction; *Buffalo Jump: A Woman's Travels* (Coteau, 1999, winner of the Hubert Evans Award for Non-Fiction and the VanCity Book Prize); *The Windshift Line* (Greystone, 2005, shortlisted for the Hubert Evans Award); and *The Third Crop:*

A Personal and Historical Journey into the photo albums and shoe boxes of the Slocan Valley, 1800s to early 1940s (Sono Nis, 2011, Honourable Mention in the Lieutenant-Governor's Medal for Historical Writing). Her work appears in anthologies such as *Nobody's Mother* (TouchWood); *Going Some Place* (Coteau); *Sleds, Sleighs and Snow* (Whitecap); *75 Readings Plus* (Mc-Graw-Hill Ryerson); *Genius of Place* (Polestar); and magazines such as *Borealis*. She has served as juror for numerous literary competitions, and recently edited several books, including Lee Reid's *Growing Home: the Legacy of Kootenay Elders* and *Growing Together: Conversations with Seniors and Youth*. Moir has worked or lived in Brandon, Manitoba; Lethbridge, Alberta; Fargo, North Dakota; Freeport, Nova Scotia; St. Paul, Minnesota; Amherst, Massachusetts; Sudbury, Ontario; Prince Rupert, Nelson, and Vancouver, British Columbia. She shares her home in Vallican with her partner, Dan, their cat, Lida Rose Chutney, and dog, Brier.